SARA HINES MARTIN

Contains Workbook Activities

BROADMAN PRESS
Nashville, Tennessee

ISBN: 0-8054-6010-1
Dewey Decimal Classification: 616.86
Subject Heading: ALCOHOLISM
Library of Congress Catalog Card Number: 89-17425

Printed in the United States of America

Unless otherwise indicated, Scripture quotations are from the *King James Version* of the Bible. Scripture quotations marked (NIV) are from the Holy Bible, *New International Version,* copyright © 1973, 1978, 1984 by International Bible Society. Scripture quotations marked (TLB) are from *The Living Bible.* Copyright © Tyndale House Publishers, Wheaton, Illinois, 1971. Used by permission.

The Friel Co-Dependency Assessment Inventory in Chapter 1 is from John C. Friel and Linda D. Friel, *Adult Children: The Secrets of Dysfunctional Families* (Deerfield Beach, Fla.: Health Publications, 1988). Used by permission of the authors. Graphs in Chapter 2 are from THE GRIEF RECOVERY HANDBOOK by John James and Frank Cherry. Copyright © 1988 by John James and Frank Cherry. Reprinted by permission of Harper & Row, Publishers, Inc.

The recovery chart in Chapter 10 is from Dene T. Stamas, "New Attitudes," Changing Self Defeating Attitudes of Adult Children of Alcoholics (Lombard, Ill.: Adult Children Center, 1988). Used by permission.

Library of Congress Cataloging-in-Publication Data

Martin, Sara Hines, 1933-
  Shame on you! / Sara Hines Martin.
    p.   cm.
  Includes bibliographical references.
  ISBN 0-8054-6010-1
  1. Adult children of alcoholics.   2. Self-help techniques.
I. Title.
HV5132.M363 1990
362.23'23–dc20   89-17425
                                                                        CIP

Prayer for Serenity

God, grant me the serenity to accept the things I cannot change, courage to change the things I can, and wisdom to know the difference;

Living one day at a time, enjoying one moment at a time;

Accepting hardship as a pathway to peace; taking, as Jesus did, this sinful world as it is, not as I would have it;

Trusting that You will make all things right if I surrender to Your will;

So that I may be reasonably happy in this life and supremely happy with You forever in the next. AMEN

Reinhold Niebuhr

Preface

"Shame on you!"

"You should be ashamed of yourself!"

How often did you hear that type of statement from parents and other authority figures as you grew up? How often did you receive shaming statements? Martha, forty-five, still hears her father say at family and community gatherings, "My wife cheated me. She gave me four girls and only one son." According to Martha's viewpoint, Daddy always elevated the son like a prince and valued him much more highly than he did his daughters. What Daddy, now nearly eighty, does not know is that the brother, at fourteen, had sex with Martha several times when she was nine. "It would break Daddy's heart if I ever told him, so I have kept quiet all these years." Daddy's comment and the incest still carry the power to make Martha feel ashamed of who she is.

This book deals with the way families can become shame-bound, producing shame-based individuals.

Parental behavior will be discussed in the book, but the emphasis of this book is on *the feelings children have* rather than *what parents did*. It is about *us,* not *them*. Feelings of hurt and loss can take place within the child even though the parent did not engage in abusive behavior. A father goes away for extended military service; a parent goes into an institution for mental illness; a parent dies—these experiences bring a deep sense of loss. Elliot, now sixty, went to live with Grandmother at age four when Mommy went into the hospital for major surgery. Possibly Mommy explained things fully to her young son, but he felt that his beloved mother had given him away.

Beth Polson and Miller Newton say in *Not My Kid* that parents don't have to *do* something to cause children to have negative feelings about themselves and life. Parents who do not have good feelings about their own lives probably communicate those feelings to their children every day. "And the child who watches a parent feel bad about life may feel bad about life himself."

John Sandford talks about parents who were in a crisis situation—perhaps economic—at the time the children were being born. The parents may have sincerely wanted their children, but they could have felt unwanted due to what was going on in the family at that time. Those children could have wounded feelings.

Sometimes severely abusive behavior took place. Jane Middelton-Moz writes, *Children of trauma are most frequently children of parents who themselves experienced trauma that was never resolved.* Theodore Rubin says, "We are victims of victims."

"All children experience trauma of one kind or another before reaching the age of 18," according to Middelton-Moz. Alice Miller says, "It is not the traumas we suffer in childhood which make us emotionally ill but the inability to express the trauma."

"The damage to a child's sense of self occurs less through the experience of the trauma itself than the reaction by the adults in that child's life after the fact," states Middelton-Moz. Robert Subby says, "The presence of a trauma such as alcoholism is not so important as the operational rules of the system." Thus damage to children of trauma occurs to a large extent because the parents lack skills for helping the children resolve the trauma.

John Bradshaw concludes that any person raised in a family of trauma becomes *shame-based.* "Children of trauma experience too much stimulus within a short period of time to be able to adequately master that stimulus." That brings on *toxic shame* which he calls "soul murder."

A person becomes shame-bound when he receives messages that make him feel ashamed at any time that he feels any feeling, need, or drive. Bradshaw says,

> Shame has been called the master emotion because as it is internal-

ized, all other emotions are bound by shame. Most of our spontaneous instinctual life gets shamed. Children are shamed for being too rambunctious, for wanting things, and for laughing too loud. Children are forced to eat when they are not hungry (and are shamed if they don't want to eat).

When our instinctual life is shamed, it's like an acorn going through agony for becoming an oak, or a flower feeling ashamed for blossoming.

He talks about how good children are defined: meek, considerate, unselfish, and perfectly law-abiding. Parents make rules to curb spontaneity. These rules then cause even well-intentioned parents to abandon their children. This abandonment creates toxic shame. He points out that parents cannot teach their children self-valuing if they themselves are shame-based.

I use the term *Adult Child* generically. An Adult Child is a person who grew up in a shame-bound family. He or she has probably achieved normal height and weight for a grown-up. He or she has acquired a full command of the language. He or she has acquired vocational and mental skills and works in an occupation befitting a grown-up. The surface appearance and behaviors speak of adulthood, but underneath is a child who is angry, scared, hurt, and sad.

In this book we talk about how to cut loose from that shame and move on to wholeness.

All names used except those of professionals are fictitious.

Contents

1
Letting Go of the Shame

A couple of years ago, I took to my private counselor a list of all the crises and traumas, ranging from surgery to an accidental fall to the results of unwise decisions, that had happened within my immediate family that year. "Why can't things settle down?" I asked. "What is going on that something is always taking place to gobble up our money, drain our emotional resources, and devour our time?"

"How did you feel after each episode?" she asked.

"Ashamed," I answered.

"Exactly," she concurred. "When we have an inner core of shame, we keep on doing things that perpetuate that shame. The only way to stop this cycle is to let go of the feeling of shame."

In the fall of 1988 I spent a week at a co-dependency treatment center for my personal growth. I joined a group of four other persons led by two cotherapists. Our primary task was to work on letting go of our shame. When I arrived, to my surprise, a feeling of shame descended upon me. I had written a book for Adult Children of Alcoholics and am a counselor who specializes in working with that population; therefore, I should be cured! I handled the matter in a style befitting my Adult Child identity: I decided I would keep my professions secret. When introducing myself, I simply said, "I am a writer."

We started work on Monday morning. On Tuesday evening, I conducted a dialogue with myself. "This secrecy is affecting your getting the maximum benefit out of this event." After some inner struggle, I said, "OK, I'll take a risk. I'll tell them *who I am.*"

On Wednesday morning, I said, "I have a confession to make." It came out in a rush. "I've-written-a-book-on-Adult-Children-of-Al-coholics-and-I'm-a-counselor-who-works-with-Adult-Children-and-I'm-so-ashamed-that-I'm-not-fixed." As I started to speak, my arms clasped involuntarily over my head, to cover my feeling of shame.

That episode shows how, when we feel shame at our core, we can take even accomplishments and turn them into situations about which we feel shame.

Sources of Shame

Shame can be given to us only by authority figures: parents, teachers, ministers, and others. Shame that is not given back to parents is passed on to children. When they become adults, they do not know how to give their shame back to their parents so grandchildren act it out; and so the shame passes on from generation to generation.

Sometimes a child was shamed because he or she was the wrong sex; one parent (or both) made it plain that the child should have been a boy instead of a girl, for example. A woman has a photograph of her father at age six: his curls fall to his shoulders and he is wearing a dress. "He was the fifteenth child in a family where there had come girl, boy, girl, boy through number fourteen. It was time for a girl, but Daddy appeared. Grandmother dressed and treated Daddy as a girl."

Here are examples of statements that create shame in children:

How could you . . .
   do what you do?
   think the way you think?
   be the way you are?
Why can't you . . .
   be like your brother?
   grow up?
When I was a kid . . . .
Just do what you're told.
Everything was fine until you came along.
When I was your age, I behaved perfectly.
God will get you.

A family secret creates shame. That secret may be a traumatic event, perhaps several generations removed, which possibly no one in the present generation knows. That event has been kept secret and passed on unconsciously from generation to generation. Boundary difficulties and shame help perpetuate the secret. The family expends a large amount of energy protecting the secret. Addictive behavior results. The addiction, in turn, helps keep the shame alive. One member of each generation is "chosen" to act out the shameful behavior. Though the "choice" is unconscious on the part of parents and children, all parties accept the person's role.

The social systems, such as school and church, give additional shame messages. Children are shamed in school if they are "too" anything—too smart, too dumb, too different. Grades posted on the bulletin board reveal who received the failing grades and exposes those students to shame. The beautiful and bright students are valued most of all. What happens to those who fall into neither category?

Churches can give messages that stir up feelings of shame. Rather than creating a healthy sense of guilt, which can lead to confession and forgiveness, these messages can create an attitude of low self-worth, which leads to more shame.

Types of Shame

John Bradshaw, in *Healing the Shame that Binds You,* describes two forms of shame: *nourishing (healthy) shame* and *toxic shame. Healthy shame,* he says, is an emotion that defines our limits. We need structure and we develop boundaries to provide that structure. Healthy shame sets boundaries for us as humans. It is the emotional energy that tells us we are not God. It keeps us humble; we know we don't know it all. The person who has healthy shame has a good relationship with herself.

If a child has parents who can set firm but loving limits so that she can explore in safety and have tantrums without the parent withdrawing love, the child can develop a healthy sense of shame.

Toxic shame is the emotion that gives a person the feeling that he is defective as a human being. He views himself as an object worthy of contempt. A shame-based person resists exposing his inner self to others and to himself as well. Bradshaw says, "A shame-based person is haunted by a sense of emptiness." This process takes place when the child is so young he has not developed ego boundaries to protect himself.

The person who has toxic shame doesn't just *feel* shame; his identity is shame. He feels the need to create a false self. Jesus delivered harsh criticism against *hypocrites,* those who pretended to be something they were not. Shame-based persons act *shameless* (pass their shame on to another) by giving perfectionist messages, trying to control, criticizing and blaming, patronizing; being judgmental, being filled with rage, being arrogant, being envious, and by being people-pleasers. People who have toxic shame become addicts of one sort or another; they may use chemicals or they may develop addictive forms of behavior.

For the remainder of this book, when I speak of shame, I am referring to toxic shame.

Conditions Causing Abandonment Feelings

When a child feels abandoned by parents, his feelings become bound by shame, thus shame-bound. Bradshaw names the conditions that cause feelings of abandonment:

The Loss of Mirroring

During the first years of life, a child needs a primary parent who will take him seriously and admire him—to value him for the one-and-only human being he is. A child knows who he is only by "mirroring" from the caretaker, which means that the parent mirrors, or reflects, the child's emotions to him. In this act the parent gives strong, affirming eye contact with the child and says in a nonverbal way, "I understand what you're feeling."

Mirroring can take place when the mother (usually) has a firm sense of personal boundaries, has her own needs met in her relationship with her husband, is free enough from stress in her own life so that she can enjoy her newborn infant, has the time to hold him, and relaxes as she interacts with him. Shame-bound parents are shut down emotionally; therefore, they have difficulty mirroring and giving their children affirmation messages about their emotions.

Recently, I led a thirty-one-year-old male client through a visualization exercise dealing with mirroring. His father has been alcoholic

all this man's life and his mother has always been harried and distracted. Although she was basically kind in her treatment of her son, her
preoccupation was a major problem for him. The young man was able
to visualize Mother holding him as an infant in her arms. When I
asked, "Can you see her looking at you and giving you her total
attention?"

"No," he said, "she's distracted."

Neglect of Developmental Dependency Needs

A child has tremendous dependency needs; he depends on his
parents to meet those needs. Parents who have experienced trauma
often are not able or available to supply needed nurture. These parents
may give their child shaming messages for expressing his needs, and
the child feels shame for having needs.

Abuse of Any Type

Emotional abuse takes place when parents say or imply that emotions are weak and that the child must repress any expression of her
primary emotions: sadness, fear, anger, guilt, shame, joy.

Verbal abuse takes place when parents hurt with words: call the
child names, use a tone of voice that cuts, uses words to reject or
humiliate a child, and so forth. *Physical abuse* occurs when a parent
hits a child to vent his or her own anger with the primary motive of
hurting the child rather than teaching him. *Sexual abuse* creates the
greatest amount of shame in the child. It takes less sexual abuse to
bring shame than any other type of abuse. Physical abuse ranks
second.

Enmeshment

Enmeshment into the needs (conscious or unconscious) of the parents or the family system needs can cause feelings of abandonment.
Individuals from shame-bound families often match up with others
from similar families. When this matching happens, the husband and
wife are not able to meet each other's emotional needs, thus are not
able to meet the child's needs. When she feels needy, she is shamed
because her needs clash with the adults' needs. That process makes

the child become an Adult Child—a child who acts like an adult when young and who remains a child when grown-up.

Adult Children act out in their marriages the unresolved shame from their homes. A man who had been sexually abused by his mother got married but then felt shame when he had sex with his wife.

Some Shame Issues

Bradshaw refers to seven basic issues within a shame-bound family system:

1. Control—Control is the major defense strategy for shame.

2. Denial of the Five Freedoms—The power to perceive; to think and interpret; to feel; to want and choose; the power to imagine.

3. Blame—Blame is a defensive cover-up for shame.

4. Perfectionism—No one ever measures up.

The perfectionist rule says, "You shouldn't perceive, think, feel, desire, or imagine the way you do. You should do these the way the perfectionistic ideal demands."

5. The No-Talk Rule—In shame-bound families, members want to hide their true feelings, needs, or wants.

6. Don't Make Mistakes—Cover up your own mistakes and if anyone else makes a mistake, shame him.

7. Unreliability—Don't expect reliability in relationships. Don't trust anyone and you will never be disappointed.

Results of Toxic Shame

Toxic shame causes one to reject oneself. A conference leader said, "We focus so much on the ways our parents abandoned us that we lose sight of the fact that we abandon ourselves." We give ourselves away; we do not take up for ourselves; we give our personal power away; we do things that bring self-destruction.

Bradshaw says that the final result of toxic shame is *spiritual bankruptcy.* He says, "We are not material beings on a spiritual journey; we are spiritual beings who need an earthly journey to become fully spiritual." He quotes a Spanish philosopher who says that man is the only being who lives from within, who has an inner self. Jesus said, "The kingdom of heaven is within you." Toxic shame causes the person to look outside for reassurance that he is worthwhile since he views his inside as defective.

Respectful and Shame-Bound Family Systems

Merle Fossum and Marilyn Mason list two types of family systems in *Facing Shame: Families in Recovery*

1. Respectful—

• Clear personal boundaries between family members;

• Accountability (such as taking responsibility for one's feelings rather than saying, "You make me angry," and calling on members to be accountable for their behavior rather than other members protecting them and enabling them to continue those behaviors);

• Growing closeness (empathy);

• Development of people in person-to-person relationships as whole persons.

2. Shame-bound—

• Vague personal boundaries;

• Perfectionism rather than accountability (much blaming but much rescuing);

• The system grows increasingly rigid, and parents grow more controlling. Family members become increasingly alienated from one another.

• Confused boundaries (which keep family members from having close interaction) result.

• Perfectionism results.

Types of Shame-Bound Families

In *Lost in the Shuffle,* Robert Subby lists four types of shame-bound families which produce shame-based individuals:

1. Those with alcoholism and chemical dependency;

2. Emotionally or psychologically disturbed family systems;

3. Physically/sexually abusive families;

4. Rigid religious or dogmatic families.

In a rigid religious family, parents overcontrol children. "They offer family members only a one-dimensional view of the world—a view that stresses order, discipline, regimentation, and, above all, *sameness.* Children grow up to be little sergeants," Subby says.

Guilt Versus Shame

How does shame differ from guilt? Fossum and Mason define shame as "an inner sense of being completely diminished or insufficient as a person." The person feels badly about *himself.* Guilt on the other hand, focuses on behaviors and values. It is more mature. Fossum and Mason describe guilt as "the painful feeling of regret a person has about behavior that has violated a personal value." It develops later than shame, after the age of three. If a person is capable of experiencing guilt, he has developed some inner rules and a conscience. *One can feel badly about behavior but can still respect oneself.*

Guilt is about what I do, *behavior.* I can change behavior. If I tell a lie, I can stop lying.

Shame is about *me*—who I am, *personhood.* It is perceived as failure. The person feels hopeless, doomed forever.

Guilt is a fault of *doing.*

Shame is a fault of *being.*

Guilt involves a choice.

Shame is involuntary.

With guilt, people count.

With shame, objects count.

Guilt has an internal judge. We develop our own sense of values and say, "I can change what I'm doing because that violates my moral code."

Shame has an external judge. We give others the power to judge us. *"What would others think?"*

Guilt responds proportionately to the action.

Shame is disproportionate to the act, overwhelming. A trivial event can trigger a massive feeling of shame. We get a "shame attack," or our "shame albums" in our minds open and replay every shameful thing we have ever done.

Guilt focuses on specifics: "You told a lie."

Shame focuses on persons: "You are a liar." This position defines the person in his totality as a liar and does not recognize other parts of himself. Even the person who tells many lies may occasionally tell the truth.

Guilt: "You did a bad act."

Shame: "You are a bad person."

Guilt: "What did I *do?*"

Shame: "What did *I* do?"

Guilt: "Why did you do *that?*"

Shame: "Why did *you* do that?"

Once shame becomes a part of a person, it is a *primary* effect; it overrides all other feelings. We think we're unspeakably bad. Shame becomes rage (the appropriate human response to abuse). It is difficult for a shamed person to relate to self, the other sex, or God.

Shame Messages

In a shame-bound system, these messages—overt or hidden—are given that keep people locked into shame.

You don't have the right to be yourself.

You don't have the right to share your pain.

You don't have the right to heal, to be whole.

When we share our pain, we get *should* messages.

"You shouldn't talk."

"You shouldn't feel."

Once you're shamed for sharing the pain, every time you feel that pain in the future, shame comes right behind. If someone is shamed for having feelings of any type or for doing a specific type of behavior, such as sexual feelings or behavior, shame comes whenever the person has sexual feelings or behavior.

Shame and Co-Dependency

Bradshaw says, "Internalized shame is the essence of co-dependency." Co-Dependency results in several typical behavior patterns. The following list is based on material written by Gail Rekers and John Hipple.

Co-Dependents have a high tolerance for inappropriate behavior. Occasionally they will break out of that pattern and take a stand for themselves. Usually they feel guilty about speaking up and revert to tolerating intolerable behavior.

Co-Dependents look outside themselves for validation that they are worthwhile human beings and that what they are doing is right.

They focus on being "responsible for" people they care about rather than being "responsible to."

They look adult, act "put together," have "surface maturity."

They are confused about intimate and sexual roles.

They are "other-ated"; they observe another's performance and not their own.

They distort relationships, either by maximizing similarities or minimizing differences.

They value self-neglect as an ideal state desirable in a relationship.

Subby says: "Co-dependency can emerge from any family system where certain overt and covert rules exist—rules that interfere with the normal process of the emotional, psychological, behavioral and spiritual development. Rules interfere with healthy growth and make constructive change very difficult, if not impossible."

Letting Go of the Shame

Family members often think, *If the alcoholic (or whatever) would leave, everything would be all right.* The alcoholic can leave, but the shame stays. An alcoholic father left home, and the mother started sexually abusing their five-year-old son. The shame continued.

The way to get rid of the shame is to give it back to our parents. *We don't blame them; we hold them responsible.* When we give back their shame, we make them responsible. Until we give it back, we're enablers; we help them to be irresponsible. A pastoral counselor said, "My addicted father didn't go into treatment because I carried the shame for him. When I gave him back his shame, he entered treatment." Parents will not volunteer to take back the shame, so the child must initiate giving it back.

Giving back the shame is about *you,* not about the other. The shame needs to go *out* of the victim, not necessarily *back* to the abuser. He or she doesn't need to be present for the victim to do the work. (The abuser may be dead.) Giving back shame may work more effectively with a therapist and/or a support group. You need to have other people to help you—people who can identify and hear you nonjudgmentally.

You *can* get rid of your shame. In the chapters that follow we'll explore ways to help you let go of the shame.

Activities

Write in this book or use a separate notebook.

Clues of Shame

A person may ask, "How do I know if I am shame-bound"? Here are some clues.

1. Do you have "frozen speech" (real difficulty expressing yourself)?
2. Do you feel an urgency to hide?
3. Do you have a profound sense of loneliness?
4. Do you think others can see inside you, read your mind?
5. Do you stay compulsively busy?
6. Do you feel weary all the time?
7. Do you feel isolated and are you perhaps socially and professionally isolated?
8. Do you have a small range of feelings and find it hard to identify a variety of feelings?

Styles of Coping with Shame

These three styles of coping with shame can vaccillate or change from one to the other. Which are your styles?

1. **Fight**—Become angry, filled with rage; feel a need to control.
2. **Flee**—Become indifferent, withdrawn, emotionally distant; feel panic, feel a need to run; change the subject when a threatening topic comes up.
3. **Freeze**—Become immobilized, depressed, numb.

Circle of Shame

Draw a circle within a larger circle. Label the core "Fear of abandonment." Label the outer circle "Shame." This drawing depicts what often takes place within a shame-bound person.

Acting Shameless

Reread the section about acting shameless—passing on one's shame to others. To what extent do you do that? To whom?

_____

_____

When we give shame messages to others, especially to our children, we need to say, "I'm sorry I shamed you."

Giving Back Your Shame

1. Decide where it came from.

List every feeling of shame you have: about your looks, your personality, your behavior, your sexuality, and so forth.

Look at your family of origin. Compile a list of the shameful feelings you *perceived* your parents have. The two lists will probably match. Your parents didn't know how to give back their shame to *their* parents, so unintentionally, they passed it on to you.

2. You must own your shame; stop denying that it is there. Share it. Until you get in touch with it, you can't give it back.

You need to say to nonjudgmental listeners, "I hurt. I'm sad. I'm sick." You need to have listeners who you take back to the place and time you were shamed, back where you said you'd never go again. We need human beings to help heal our shame since it came to us through human beings.

By sharing your feelings with others, you can challenge the rules that say, "You must not feel; you must not share."

3. Relive the trauma that produced the shame from your

present position of strength and not as the powerless child you were when you received the shame messages.

4. Get in touch with the anger you feel because you were shamed. From anger and rage, we get the gift of strength. Use that rage as strength to return the shame. This type of exercise is best done under the guidance of a professional therapist.

Therapists sometimes have a client use a foam bat, scream, or express his feelings in other ways.

A client might say, "Mother, I'm angry with you and I need to give you back your shame. I know you didn't mean to pass on your shame to me; I know you didn't know how to get rid of it, but I'm still angry."

The person can locate shame in the body: it resides in the "gut"; he can follow its path up through the stomach until it comes out of the throat. The therapist can ask during the process, "Where is your shame now?" and the person can identify the location: in the chest, throat, or no longer inside.

After returning it, the person most likely will feel empty, hollow.

5. Rebuild boundaries that have been violated by the one(s) who shamed you.

Victims have boundary problems. They can't say no to people. Once boundaries have been violated, others can violate them more easily. It's time now to build new boundaries.

Join a twelve-step group. These groups give the greatest help available for healing shame.

Take the following inventory. Mark in the book or number 1 to 60 on a sheet of paper. Answer *True* or *False* to each statement. This test reveals the degree of codependency you possess.

Friel Co-dependency Assessment Inventory

The following questions deal with how you feel about yourself, your life, and those around you. As you answer each question, be sure to answer honestly, but do not spend too much time on any one question. There are no right or wrong answers. Take each questions as it comes, and answer as you usually feel.

1. I make enough time to do things just for myself each week.
2. I spend lots of time criticizing myself after an interaction with someone.
3. I would not be embarrassed if people knew certain things about me.
4. Sometimes I feel like I just waste a lot of time and don't get anywhere.
5. I take good enough care of myself.
6. It is usually best not to tell someone they bother you; it only causes fights and gets everyone upset.
7. I am happy about the way my family communicated when I was growing up.
8. Sometimes I don't know how I really feel.
9. I am very satisfied with my intimate love life.
10. I've been feeling tired lately.
11. When I was growing up, my family liked to talk openly about problems.
12. I often look happy when I am sad or angry.
13. I am satisfied with the number and kind of relationships I have in my life.
14. Even if I had the time and money to do it, I would feel uncomfortable taking a vacation by myself.
15. I have enough help with everything that I must do each day.
16. I wish that I could accomplish a lot more than I do now.
17. My family taught me to express feelings and affection openly when I was growing up.
18. It is hard for me to talk to someone in authority (boss, teachers, etc.).
19. When I am in a relationship that becomes too confusing and complicated, I have no trouble getting out of it.
20. I sometimes feel pretty confused about who I am and where I want to go with my life.
21. I am satisfied with the way that I take care of my own needs.
22. I am not satisfied with my career.
23. I usually handle my problems calmly and directly.

24. I hold back my feelings most of the time because I don't want to hurt other people or have them think less of me.
25. I don't feel like I'm "in a rut" very often.
26. I am not satisfied with my friendships.
27. When someone hurts my feelings or does something that I don't like, I have little difficulty telling him about it.
28. When a close friend or relative asks for my help more than I'd like, I have little difficulty telling them about it.
29. I love to face new problems and am good at finding solutions to them.
30. I do not feel good about my childhood.
31. I am not concerned about my health a lot.
32. I often feel like no one really knows me.
33. I feel calm and peaceful most of the time.
34. I find it difficult to ask for what I want.
35. I don't let people take advantage of me more than I'd like.
36. I am dissatisfied with at least one of my close relationships.
37. I make major decisions quite easily.
38. I don't trust myself in new situations as much as I'd like.
39. I am very good at knowing when to speak up, and when to go along with others' wishes.
40. I wish I had more time away from my work.
41. I am as spontaneous as I'd like to be.
42. Being alone is a problem for me.
43. When someone I love is bothering me, I have no problem telling them so.
44. I often have so many things going on at once that I'm really not doing justice to any one of them.
45. I am very comfortable letting others into my life and revealing "the real me" to them.
46. I apologize to others too much for what I do or say.
47. I have no problem telling people when I'm angry with them.
48. There's so much to do and not enough time. Sometimes I'd like to leave it all behind me.
49. I have few regrets about what I have done with my life.
50. I tend to think of others more than I do myself.

51. More often than not, my life has gone the way that I wanted it to.
52. People admire me because I'm so understanding of others, even when they do something that annoys me.
53. I am comfortable with my own sexuality.
54. I sometimes feel embarrassed by behaviors of those close to me.
55. The important people in my life know "the real me," and I am OK with them knowing.
56. I do my share of work, and often do quite a bit more.
57. I do not feel that everything would fall apart without my efforts and attention.
58. I do too much for other people and then later wonder why I did so.
59. I am happy about the way my family coped with problems when I was growing up.
60. I wish that I had more people to do things with.

This inventory covers the following areas of co-dependent concerns:

1. self-care
2. self-criticism
3. secrets
4. "stuck-ness"
5. boundary issues
6. family of origin
7. feelings identification
8. intimacy
9. physical health
10. autonomy
11. over-responsibility/burnout
12. identity

Care should be taken in interpreting test scores at this time, and as with all testing, clinical interviews and impressions should be relied upon. The inventory is very useful, as is, to help focus on areas which may be troublesome and to use as a jumping-off point for setting goals for recovery.

Scoring: *Reverse all odd-numbered answers.* Thus, if you answered *True,* reverse it to *False.* Then count the total number of *True* answers to get your score. Scores below 20 indicate few co-dependent concerns; 21-30 show mild/moderate; 31-45 moderate/severe; and over 45, severe.

"What do I do if I score a high number on this test?" you ask. You could be helped by getting into a twelve-step program. Call a local Al-Anon office and ask for Adult Children's groups. Private therapy with someone who knows Adult Children's issues would be very helpful. These two approaches can supplement each other.

If you would like to receive treatment from a co-dependency treatment center (one week or a twenty-eight-day program), contact a local counselor who works in the field of Co-Dependency.

2
Letting Go of the Grief

"Most of the stress and pressure in life have to do with grief, yet it is what we're least prepared to cope with. Keeping grief inside is the cause of the majority of the pain you feel," say John James and Frank Cherry in *The Grief Recovery Handbook.* "Every grief experience not dealt with has a cumulative opposing effect on your aliveness and spontaneity. It's this accumulation that has kept life from being the joyous experience you want it to be."

Unresolved grief festers like a deep wound covered by scar tissue. Wayne Kritsberg says that when we do not discharge the energy that a loss stirs up within us, the stress builds up to a state of chronic distress which he calls chronic shock.

The Broad Scope of Grief

James and Cherry point out that other events besides death can cause grief. "*Any occasion in which you experienced a loss of trust brings a grief reaction.* Grief follows any major change in a familiar pattern of behavior." We grieve the loss of all significant emotional relationships. We grieve the loss of innocence of any type. Whenever we experience shock or have a blow to our self-esteem, we feel grief.

Ted's alcoholic father constantly spanked him for things he didn't do. Even though Ted told Dad he was innocent, Dad punished his son anyway. Ted's faith in Dad diminished. He learned not to trust. Not trusting hurt, yet that process protected him from further pain. Ted carried this expectation into life, distrusting anyone who hurt him, thereby making trust more difficult, reinforcing the cycle.

In *Healing the Child Within,* Charles Whitfield says, "A trauma is a *loss,* whether a real or threatened one. We experience a loss when we are deprived of or have to go without something that we have had and valued, something that we needed, wanted or expected."

Jane Middelton-Moz says, "The quiet 'little deaths' of everyday existence are mourned as much as those of resounding magnitude, for grief makes no comparisons nor judgments and has no understanding of degree."

"Children need their parents' time, attention, direction, and modeling," Bradshaw says. "When these needs are not met, these lost needs have to be grieved."

Here are some specific examples of incidents that cause grief because the person feels a loss of the loved, comfortable, and familiar or because he experiences shock.

- A family moves and a child loses a house, friends and pets
- A pet dies
- A person divorces or his parents divorce
- Marriage changes a familiar life-style
- Addictions bring major grief for the addict and the family
- A person retires
- A friendship breaks up
- A romance breaks up
- A person loses a limb or other body part
- A child, sibling, or spouse dies
- Someone takes legal action against a person
- Older children leave home
- Death of a dream
- A person loses his culture through social change, such as the experience of the American Indian

Importance of Resolving Grief

"Grief is the process that finishes things and allows us to move on with our life," Bradshaw says.

Avoiding grief uses as much energy as grieving the loss or trauma. "An ungrieved loss remains forever alive in our unconscious, which has no sense of time," says Whitfield. We must grieve to grow from each experience of loss. When we are not allowed to remember, to express our feelings, and to grieve or mourn our losses or traumas, whether real or threatened, through the free expression of our Child Within, we become ill, Whitfield says.

Unresolved grief begins with mild symptoms of grief and can progress to Co-Dependence and to Post Traumatic Stress Disorder. The heart of the Post Traumatic Stress Syndrome is delayed grief. Some of the symptoms of PTSS are: having feelings of unreality and panic; having nightmares and sleeping disorders; having a need to control; being easily startled; and being numbed-out psychically.

Unresolved grief can result in emotional symptoms ranging from anxiety to feelings of emptiness. A person may have somatic complaints, such as difficulty sleeping; or the result may be mental, emotional, or physical illness. *The person who does not grieve in a complete and healthy way pays a price.* Adults who have not grieved for childhood losses may become involved in behaviors that are destructive to themselves or others.

Lorie Dwinnell summarizes three possible outcomes for survivors of trauma.

1. Some people succumb. They commit suicide; they go insane or become criminal and stay in an institution much of their lives—unable to feel hopeful about themselves or to move beyond their self-defeating behavior.

2. Another group uses tremendous amounts of denial, repression, and projections. They function, but oftentimes in a limited way. They are fragile personalities who have difficulty coping when the demands on their lives exceed their level of personal skills.

3. Those who survive effectively re-experience the pain of the original trauma and work through it.

Whenever we do not adequately mourn a loss, the grief accumulates, say James and Cherry. We then feel less alive. The world starts to look like a hostile place to us. Bottled up feelings caused by loss can last a lifetime and bring a person to serious and hurtful consequences, such as abuse of another person, divorce, and emotional problems for the sufferer.

Blocks to Resolving Grief

Whitfield says that when someone feels a loss or a trauma, whether real or threatened, and if the people around him say feelings must not be expressed, *the person feels that he caused the loss or trauma.* He then feels guilty and ashamed. So what does he do? He usually blocks out the feelings by becoming *numb.*

According to Whitfield, people may learn to make other choices as they grow older:

1. To hold grief in until the person cannot stand it any longer;

2. To "stuff it" and become physically or emotionally ill, and/or explode;

3. Use alcohol or other drugs to blot out the pain;

4. Find people who will give a safe, supportive setting where one can talk about one's pain and work through it.

James and Cherry say that one of our great gifts as human beings is the ability to show emotion, yet society teaches us that feelings and the showing of feelings are not appropriate. When we share our grief with others, they frequently lack skills to help us deal with it. They may answer with a cliché, such as, "Well, you know, it takes time." This cliché encourages us to "ACT recovered," which reinforces for grievers the fear of showing the feelings that come from emotional pain.

The predominant response that comes when someone expresses pain over grief is an outright or implied statement that "you shouldn't have the feelings you have and you shouldn't deal with the feelings you have."

When a loved one dies, the normal and almost automatic response for a person is to feel angry at God. If such a feeling is expressed, someone will say to the griever, "You must not be angry with God."

James and Cherry write: "We've relied on intellect for years, so we search for understandable reasons for events. When we can't find one, we still feel the need to assign blame. God is a convenient place to put it. Through our own personal experience, we're convinced that God is big enough to understand our shortcomings."

In a troubled home, children usually are not allowed to grieve in a complete way when they suffer losses. They get negative messages, such as *Don't feel* and *Don't talk about it,* that block the grieving process.

Resolution requires time, human support, and expressing all feeling.

Anger and Grief Resolution

Whitfield states, "Whenever we are hurt, we usually feel angry, so to get free from mistreatment, we usually need to get angry." Anger is thus a major element in grief resolution. He says that our need to protect our parents and other authority figures from our anger blocks our grief work. Adult Children may fear that something bad will happen if we get angry with our parents. Whitfield says that this fear brings massive denial, leading to the fact that many Adult Children cannot remember 75 percent of what happened during their childhood.

In addition to denying anger, Adult Children take an appeasing approach by discounting what happened. "Yes, it was terrible, but why bother getting into it? That's in the past."

A third way of blocking anger is to wonder if we have developed a fantasy about what happened. We conclude, "It really didn't happen that way." (Usually siblings will make that statement to anyone who begins to open the door of resolution of problems from the past.)

Another way to block anger is to interpret the fourth commandment to honor the father and mother as meaning that children must never get angry at their parents.

A man told me an incident with his four-year-old son that helped him view feeling anger toward parents in a new light. The son hit him in the stomach with his fist, saying, "Daddy, I'm mad at you!"

"What trust he must have in me!" the father marveled, "to feel that free to express his anger toward me." The father then concluded, "God must be pleased with us when we trust Him enough to express honest anger toward Him. I know that, whenever I do, I come away feeling closer to God and more grateful for His love than before the incident."

Fifth, we can avoid our anger toward parents by feeling afraid that they will reject us if we show anger.

Sixth, we can feel afraid of the unknown if we express feelings, or we can be afraid of what might happen if we express feelings.

Some people push down their anger by forgiving their parent on a surface, syrupy sweet, pious level that is in no way akin to genuine forgiveness. The Adult Child can go on his way, putting the lid on his feelings, assuming he has handled his anger.

The last way that people protect their parents is to attack someone who says that the person needs to do recovery work. The Adult Child may defend the parents and deny that anything bad happened. Making peace with and forgiving parents are important, yet this process cannot be rushed. The pain and the anger must be worked through first.

How to Resolve Grief

Grief work is called work because it is that: exhausting mental and emotional labor. Time alone does not resolve grief. Middelton-Moz says, "Grief is one of the only problems in the world that will heal itself with support."

A person experiencing acute grief moves through predictable stages. First, he feels shock, anxiety, and anger. He then moves through pain, including hurt, depression, sadness, loneliness and remorse, and despair. He ends on either a positive or a negative note, depending on the intensity of the trauma, conditions around the loss, and the person's opportunity to grieve it.

James and Cherry point out that if we can express our angry feelings to a nonjudgmental hearer the anger will pass. If not, we hold onto the anger and it festers and blocks spiritual growth.

How can we move through the grief process to a place where we feel less pain and feel more alive? Since grief robs us of happiness, we need to face it and resolve it. We will then be able to help other grievers. We need to search our past and locate all the significant emotional loss experiences we have ever had. *We must find someone with whom we can grieve. Grief cannot be resolved in isolation.* Bradshaw says, "Millions of us Adult Children tried to heal ourselves alone. We went to sleep crying into our pillows or locked in the bathroom."

We need to find another person who has suffered a great amount of emotional loss and who, therefore, has patience and tolerance for another's grief. Grief is one of the only emotions that will heal itself if the griever has support.

Recording Grief

James and Cherry suggest compiling a *loss history graph*. (See end of chapter for directions.)

Here is the loss history graph that John James contributed to their book.

JOHN W. JAMES
BORN: February 16, 1944

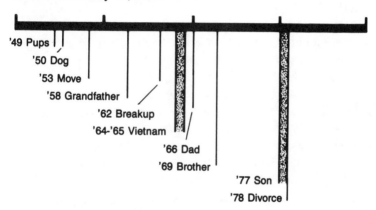

'49 Pups
'50 Dog
'53 Move
'58 Grandfather
'62 Breakup
'64-'65 Vietnam
'66 Dad
'69 Brother
'77 Son
'78 Divorce

James's earliest memory concerns the birth of puppies to the family dog in 1949. In 1950 his dog died.

In 1953 he felt unjustly punished and lost his trust in adults to a degree.

That year his family moved for the first time. Although his parents gave him rational reasons for the move, he felt sad about leaving his friends.

Several events in my family's experience illustrate the grief that can come from moving away and leaving friends. My husband and I lived overseas during the growing-up years of our children. (All three were preschool age when we first moved.) Our girls experienced a great deal of sadness about the many moves back and forth from overseas to the U.S. for furlough years every fifth year. This involved changing residences and cultures, starting new schools, leaving friends, losing pets, and changing routines.

Overseas, the school system was quite different from the one in the U.S. We had to transport our children to school because there were no school buses. Getting used to buses involved a big change. The girls took sack lunches because the schools had no lunchrooms, so they had no experience in taking money to school (and keeping up with it!). Overseas we had lived in a predominantly black culture, and on our return moved into a city that was caught in the midst of school desegration. The racial attitudes gave our children one of the greatest shocks of all.

At the end of our first furlough, in Winston-Salem, North Carolina, we cleaned out the house, packed the car, and headed into Virginia to my mother's home. Our youngest daughter, then six, had become very close friends with Mary Ann. About an hour out of town, our daughter realized that we had *left!* Because my husband and I knew fully that we were *leaving,* it did not occur to me that we had not communicated this adequately to the children or that perhaps the youngest had not understood. (It was typical for me to overexplain something to the children, yet sometimes I would do the opposite and assume they knew what was underway because it was strongly on my agenda.) Our daughter was distraught and started crying. "But I didn't get to tell Mary Ann good-bye!" How helpful it would have been if she could have taken care of that and brought the friendship to a conclusion with appropriate farewells.

When we returned to Trinidad, she was looking forward to renewing her relationship with Rosalind, her best friend in that country. We learned that Rosalind's family was due to go to England on a three-month leave, so soon after our return our daughter experienced a new grief. We were sitting in church the night that the other family had flown out. My daughter started weeping silently. "I'm missing Rosalind," she said. Producing pencil and paper, I suggested that she draw a picture of Rosalind in the plane. Since my daughter liked to draw, this appealed to her. She drew a plane with Rosalind sitting by the window with tears falling from her eyes. That exercise helped her feel better.

To return to the loss history graph, in 1958 James's grandfather died. In 1962 he and his girl friend broke up. His Vietnam experience, he says, is the one remaining unresolved grief issue in his life. In 1966, his alcoholic father died. In 1969 his younger brother died suddenly and inexplicably at age twenty. In 1977 James's son was born prematurely and died. He and his wife did not know how to handle their grief, and their relationship began to deteriorate. In 1978, he and his wife divorced. He says, "We were newly married, new parents, and new grievers at the same time. The death of our son was the straw that broke the camel's back." While he was writing *The Grief Recovery Handbook,* he called his former wife to talk about that experience. She was astonished to learn that the death of their son had affected him as strongly as it had. "How could she have known?" he asks. "I was an ACADEMY AWARD griever then."

A *relationship graph* is proposed to deal with a loss due to a death. This is the one James prepared after the death of his brother. He listed positive experiences above the line, negative experiences below it. (See end of chapter for directions to prepare such a chart.)

James recorded the date of his brother's birth in 1949. In 1956 his brother broke his bow and arrow after James had told the boy to leave them alone. In 1958 the brother crawled into bed with his older brother when the parents were fighting and the younger boy was terrified. In 1962 the younger brother helped give a going-away party for James when he went into military service.

In 1964 James told the younger brother, then fifteen, not to use his car. The boy did anyway and wrecked it. In 1965 James felt proud of how his brother had grown when James returned from service. In 1967 the brothers lived together in California, so the lines go both up and down. It was basically a happy time, but they had one big fight. In 1969 his brother called Jame on the phone while on a trip with friends. He died that afternoon.

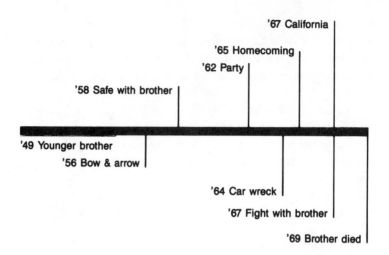

A person who has experienced loss must deal with feelings of grief. James and Cherry suggest choosing a partner who can hear you out. It is better if the partner is also dealing with grief. Meet several times, up to one hour each time, and listen to each other and cry with each other. This partner can be a therapist or the members of a support group who can hear you unconditionally.

Whitfield says that we need to tell our story which includes three parts: "What we were like," "what happened," and "what we are like now." Repeating a story gives relief to the speaker and helps him accept the reality of the loss and brings healing to the sufferer. This retelling may take a long time.

For some individuals, telling their stories allows them to recognize for the first time that abuse took place and that they feel angry about it. My young female client whose older brothers, under the direction of the father, teased her constantly, told her story for nine months in a group. A young man in the group expressed anger toward her because she dwelt on the story rather than getting into feelings, but it took her that long to acknowledge that her father and brothers had abused her and to begin to feel angry about it.

Telling the story to sympathetic listeners gives the teller freedom from the pain. He can then put the grief into perspective. When a grief is fresh, the griever focuses almost entirely on that experience and he wonders if he will ever move past it. When healthy grief work takes place, the grief shifts into a more balanced position within the person's life.

The person is now able to integrate the experience and learn from it. Herb felt devastated when he got fired from a job that paid well and which he enjoyed. After moving through the grief process, he could say, "I've learned a lot. I missed red flags all over the place. Missing those helped bring me down. I have better tools for dealing effectively in the workplace in the future."

As you work through grief, the Child Within heals and you can grow.

Completing Recovery

James and Cherry say that we need to offer forgiveness to make our recovery successful. Here are things we need to remember about forgiveness:

Others have erroneous beliefs, just as we do;

Everyone makes mistakes, just as we do;

We must forgive others in order to forgive ourselves.

These writers say that the transgressions committed against us by others fall into two categories: *real* or *imagined.*

Imagined transgressions take place when we give others the right to hurt us (such as when we did an inadequate job of communicating which helped bring about the hurt). *Real transgressions* usually happened before adult life and typically include physical violence or emotional deprivation. The transgressor was mentally or emotionally ill or he would not have abused the victim. Abusive parents are emotionally ill. Molesters are ill. *We need to forgive the sick part of the person.* We begin to make headway when we sort out the illness from the person himself.

Holding onto hurt and anger are destructive to you. "You've suffered enough from these situations," say James and Cherry. "It's now time to forgive the illnesses and let them go."

Letting Go of the Grief

To find healing, we must resolve our grief. With time and support to work through our feelings of anger and pain, resolution comes. Bradshaw assures us that when we complete the grief work, we will feel more alive and produce new and more creative behaviors. We can become an "Adult adult" rather than an Adult Child.

Activities

Loss History Graph

On a horizontal, legal-size sheet of paper, draw a line across the page and divide it into four equal parts. Record the date of your first memory (happy or sad) at the far left end. Place this year's date at the right end. Write every experience of loss you can remember even if it seems trivial at the moment. Draw a downward line for each event. The length of the line indicates the severity of the loss.

To prepare a relationship graph, draw lines above to indicate happy experiences and below to indicate the unhappy ones.

Preparing Lists of Undelivered Communications

Undelivered communications bring about denial. Since we cannot correct any of this unfinished business, we deny that there is unfinished business. After identifying the incomplete emotional issues, you need to identify and communicate what you did and did not do to make it incomplete.

The first list will name positive events you did not acknowledge to the person before his death. For example: "The time you took up for me when others were criticizing me."

The second will contain negative events you did not acknowledge. For example: "You put work first ahead of the family."

The third list will give significant emotional statements you did not deliver. That includes issues you have discovered since the loss. For example, "I never told you how much I loved you." An issue discovered later might be a widow who says, "I'm angry that you told me I was taken care of financially in case you died and that isn't true."

Go through your negative lists and, if you are ready, make statements of forgiveness to the other person.

James and Cherry say that when you can say "I love you" to that person you are finished. If you can't do that, keep going. Visualize the other person and say good-bye.

3
Letting Go of the Anger

Carrying around anger feels like dragging a sack of cement all day. It impedes our progress, keeps us earthbound, and prevents our soaring. It prevents our reaching out for new experiences and relationships. It makes us feel bad physically, emotionally, socially, and spiritually. So why do we persist in holding onto something that we know with our sane selves hurts *us* more than the one against whom we hold the anger?

Learning About Anger

If someone said, "It just started raining," how would you react emotionally? Hardly at all, probably, unless the rain would upset plans to climb a mountain. My wish for Adult Children is that we could advance in our skills for coping with anger to such an extent that if someone said, "I'm feeling angry at you," our emotional gauges would rise no higher than if we heard it is raining.

Many of us have feared and avoided anger to such an extent that we take flight at a hint of annoyance in another person. A goal for Adult Children is to learn more about anger so that it will lose its power to intimidate us. From several sources, I have compiled some laws about anger that can help us understand this phenomenon and turn loose our fears about anger.

Everybody gets angry. The ways we express anger are learned.

Angry people are people who have not received the nurture they needed.

Repressed anger leads to anxiety.

Anger is energy. We can learn to channel that energy constructively.

Where there's anger, there's pain.

Anger has only the power we give it. If we can stop being intimidated by it, it will lose its power to devastate us.

Scott Peck, in *The Road Less Traveled,* says: **"Only with anger can we survive.** Without anger we would be continually stepped on, until we were totally squashed and exterminated." (Emphasis mine)

In *Daily Affirmations for Adult Children of Alcoholics,* Rokelle Lerner says: **"Anger will not kill anyone.** Emotions are not powerful enough to strike someone down." (Emphasis mine) The way some people express anger strikes people down but not the emotions themselves.

In *Coping with Your Anger: A Christian Guide,* Andrew D. Lester says:

> Anger has a poor reputation in our society, particularly in the church.
>
> The Bible takes for granted that anger is part of human nature, part of how God created us.
>
> Godly persons are those who are careful with their anger.
>
> Jesus got angry. However, he did not sin with his anger!
>
> Problems are caused when you equate anger with sin.
>
> Jesus and Paul both warn that hiding our anger is dangerous.
>
> Anger is more closely related to our spiritual lives than is commonly recognized.
>
> To deny that you experience anger would be to deny that you are finite and, in effect, claim to be like God! Share your anger with God, it will deepen your relationship.
>
> Silence and withdrawal are two of the most common means by which persons try to conceal anger.
>
> Find appropriate ways to express and resolve the anger. Ways that are loving and, if possible, lead to reconciliation.

Harriet Lerner, in *The Dance of Anger,* says:

> Anger is neither legitimate nor illegitimate, meaningful nor pointless. Anger simply is.
>
> Those who are locked into ineffective expressions of anger suffer as deeply as those who dare not get angry at all.

Guilt and self-doubt help blot out the awareness of anger.

It requires courage to know when we are angry and to let others hear about it.

Most of us have received little help in learning to use our anger to clarify and strengthen ourselves and our relationships.

We can use our anger energy in the service of our own dignity and growth.

We can use our anger to change patterns rather than blame people.

Many times, blowing up or fighting may offer temporary relief, but when the storm passes, we find that nothing has really changed.

Theodore Rubin, author of *The Angry Book,* says:

Anger is neither good nor bad.

Unexpressed anger affects us physically.

Perverted anger provides a reservoir of emotional slush that poisons one's system.

We transfer anger to safer people and objects.

We can choose to deny our anger, or we can choose to be human.

Repressed anger always exacts a price.

People who stockpile anger are in a poor position for closeness or trust.

When anger begins to be expressed constructively, relationships improve.

The greater the awareness (of your anger), the less chance there is to lose control.

The ideal: To know you're angry as soon as you get angry and be able to express your anger at once, if you so choose.

We generally get mad at people who mean something to us.

If a relationship is destroyed by a show of anger, then it was a sick, destructive one and all parties are better off for its termination.

Anger is always appropriate. It seems inappropriate only when we don't understand it.

Females get angry as well as males.

Negate anger and you must also negate love.

Angry people . . . use a lot of energy keeping their anger down.

The healthy and appropriate feeling and expressing of human emotions, and especially anger, make for an enormous contribution to mental health.

Angry feelings are the antithesis of rejection.

Feeling angry and expressing anger get easier with practice.

Albert Ellis says in *Anger: How to Live with and Without It:*

Anger stems from equating a person's actions as the person himself. We need to separate the person from the behavior. For example, we say, "She is a selfish person," rather than "She did a selfish thing."

Anger and other emotions have a tendency to increase in intensity and expand under pressure.

Anger tends to overlap into other areas of your life.

Feeling angry toward another person can protect us from acknowledging our own responsibility in our own mess. Blaming can give us a false assurance that we are doing something about our problems.

When angry, take a look at your Belief System (the Shoulds in your thinking.)"

Blocks to Releasing Anger

We saw the important adults in our lives holding onto anger, avoiding it, repressing it, or expressing it in destructive/inappropriate ways. They were our models. How many of us saw parents, other relatives, or church members talk about their angry feelings, work through them, and lay them aside? We saw marriages torn by anger (sometimes literally but often the parents continued to remain married and live in the same house); we witnessed churches split by anger and hard feelings; we observed communities divided by anger. Our role models lacked skills for expressing anger constructively.

Our anger may have served a purpose to keep us safe. Anger can protect from invasion of our boundaries, and sometimes that is the only shield that effectively keeps an invader at a distance. Gloria said, "My mother-in-law invaded my boundaries as a standard happening; I learned that the only thing that made her keep some distance was my anger. So I kept it in place like an armor."

Other emotions mixed with anger and made it difficult to sort out exactly what we were feeling.

Confusion mixed with anger. Other people told us we should not get angry, yet we saw one parent or both get angry. Why was it OK for the adults and not for us?

Fear mixed with anger. Maybe we saw the nonalcoholic parent frightened at the loud voice or swinging hand or thrown objects of the other. If the big, strong grown-up shows fear, the situation must be scary. Gloria said, "If we children started getting into a normal squabble, Mother got nervous and squelched it. I realize now that I computed that anger must be a very fearful thing. As I grew up and developed friendships, if a friend ever showed the slightest annoyance toward me, I dropped the friend because I assumed she was through with me. It took me a long time to see that people can still remain in a relationship even though anger may be present."

In other situations, fear of physical harm kept us from venting our anger.

Fear of abandonment mixed with anger. Since the fear of abandonment was present at the best of times, we felt especially concerned that the parent would leave if we ever showed disapproval or anger.

Guilt mixed with anger. When we expressed anger, someone usually said:

"You shouldn't feel angry."

"You know the Good Book says to honor your father (mother)."

"Don't you dare talk to me that way!"

"Don't talk that way about your father (mother.)"

"It hurts me so much when you talk that way to me."

"Don't get mad. Daddy's (Mother's) just drunk."

"What's the matter with *you?*"

"You know your father (mother) loves you very much."

"Take that scowl off your face."

"How can you say such a thing?"

Sadness mixed with anger. At the time, we may not have known we felt sad. We may not have known the word. It is not likely that we saw our parents express sadness, hurt, and grief in healthy ways. Since anger is a secondary emotion that follows a primary emotion, such as sadness, sadness may have been deep underneath the surface anger.

Gloria has gotten in touch with her sadness at middle age. "Resolving the anger showed me that I had had a mountain of anger on top of a sea of sadness." She has cried almost daily for the past three years. Sometimes she wonders if the sadness will go away.

Adult Children behave as children, and it is characteristic of a child to hold onto things (whether literal objects or emotions). In Transactional Analysis terms, we have a Critical Parent (the depository of all our "shoulds") and a Child (the seat of feelings). When a feeling stirs in our Child, the Child part of us has been denied the right and the necessary encouragement to exist, so it lacks skills to handle feelings in a healthy way. The Child then flips the feeling up to the Critical Parent who handles the feelings in judgmental, repressive ways. The Critical Parent puts the lid on the hurt and pushes anger to the fore. The person is then aware of anger only.

If we are to move beyond the immature style of handling feelings, we must strengthen our Child so that part of our personality can handle the primary feelings and not turn them over to the Critical Parent. That means we cry, share our feelings with a supportive hearer, confront the person who has hurt us, and turn loose the anger. That cleans out the hurt and keeps the Critical Parent from being involved.

When a child enters the toilet-training stage, he learns that he has the power to control. Children from traumatic environments usually do not progress very far beyond that developmental stage, so control remains a dominant concern. We hold onto everything, which includes anger.

Letting Go of the Anger

Letting go of anger, then, involves becoming more emotionally mature. Sometimes people have spiritual experiences in which they take giant steps toward emotional maturity; yet for the average person, basic personality is not changed by a spiritual experience. We have only to look at the numerous church splits and recall church fights in which mature persons yelled at one another, made accusations, took sides, behaved impulsively, got in power struggles, lied, gossiped, participated in character assassinations, fired leaders without thinking about how that minister's family would survive, held onto hurt feelings, refused to forgive, stopped speaking to each other, or left the church to see that many people who have been church members for years behave in ways that would be described as pre-school behavior.

A spiritual experience usually does not give one a new personality type. The apostle Paul, for example, changed from an aggressive

Christian-killer to an aggressive ambassador for Christ. His new style was tempered by love, but he did not change from a tiger to a pussycat after conversion. Becoming a Christian does not give one instant skills for dealing with one's own anger or skills in communicating anger. Conversion gives one a motivation for change and growth and places one in a setting where they can take place, but it is rare that God gives a person a new personality. We are "new creatures," born again, just that. We are newborn babes. Babies have the capacity to grow and need to grow. They are unformed and immature.

Holding onto anger has caused as much destruction within church life and the Christian community as anything else. Christians, as a whole, hold onto anger about as much as the general population.

When I taught a class in a seminary extension school, I told that Alfred Adler said that most children form their positions of viewing life at about age five and take that position with them throughout life, behaving on that level even when grown. I gave the class a personality inventory that would reveal how they saw life as a young child, and which would probably show how they handle life now.

A minister in his forties said in a belligerent and bragging style: "No way! When the Lord saved me, He made me new! I'm not still acting the way I did when I was five years old!" He disputed the viewpoint at length, confirming for me the validity of Adler's theory. That man showed little openness to a new viewpoint that one could use to thoughtfully evaluate one's maturity level and behavior. That concept is not a judgmental viewpoint; it states what happens to people in their development until they do serious personal growth work to move themselves beyond that level.

Letting go of anger means putting it aside, as one might put aside that heavy sack of cement. Unburdened, we are free to soar, to develop new relationships, to enjoy new experiences.

Activities

The following Personal Anger Inventory may help you understand your own anger and the feelings you have toward anger. Write in the book or use a separate notebook.

Personal Anger Inventory

1. Write the philosophy regarding anger from your family of origin.

_____

_____

   • Write your personal philosophy regarding anger.

_____

_____

   • What similarities/differences do you see between the two?

_____

_____

2. What messages did you receive about anger as a child?
   • From the home

_____

   • From church

_____

   • From school and society

_____

   • From other significant adults

_____

3. Did you receive any "either-or" messages in your home?
   • "Either you are talking to me all the time, or you're angry at me."
   • "Either you withhold your anger, or I will reject you."
   • "Either you withhold your anger, or I will make you feel guilty."
   • "Either you withhold your anger, or I will withhold my love."

- "Either you withhold your anger, or you don't love me."
- "Either you withhold your anger, or I will be destroyed."
- "Either you withhold your anger, or I will try to control you."
- "Either you withhold your anger, or I will attack your self-esteem."

4. In your home, was it OK for only one parent to show anger? If so, which?_____.
   - Was it OK for only one sex to show anger?
   - If so, which?_____

5. How did you know when your father was angry?

_____

_____

   - Your mother?

_____

_____

6. Were you aware of being angry as a child? If so, how did you handle it?

_____

_____

What type of reactions did this bring from others?

_____

_____

7. Create a metaphor or simile for your anger.
   Metaphor - My anger is a

_____

_____

   Simile - My anger is like a

_____

_____

8. What does your anger do *to* you?

_____

_____

   What does it do *for* you?

_____

_____

9. I express my anger by:
   - turning it inward (depression, self-hatred, etc.)
   - verbally attacking others
   - physically attacking others or hitting things
   - speaking directly to the person, using "I" statements
   - doing nothing (paralysis)

10. The way I express my anger is similar to the way my:
    _____ father
    _____ mother
    _____ other significant adult in my childhood expressed his/
her anger.

11. To what extent are you in touch with your anger?
    _____ not at all
    _____ slightly
    _____ moderately
    _____ very much

12. I am:
    _____ slightly angry
    _____ moderately angry
    _____ enraged
    _____ have mood swings (feel different at different times)

Mark your anger level on a scale of 1 to 10, with 1 being lowest,
10 being highest.

1   2   3   4   5   6   7   8   9   10

13. To what extent do you feel comfortable:
    acknowledging your anger? _____
    owning anger?   _____
    expressing anger appropriately? _____ .

14. What is your greatest need for help in relation to your anger?
    _____ getting in touch with it
    _____ owning it
    _____ expressing it appropriately

15. What do you do to keep your anger alive?
    _____ Tell it repeatedly to yourself.
    _____ Tell it repeatedly to a sympathetic friend.

_____ Keep it in (avoid thinking about it or dealing with it).

_____ Keep on allowing yourself to be victimized by the abuser.

_____ Drink or use another substance to handle it.

16. How do you punish people toward whom you feel angry?

_____ Withdraw from them.

_____ Gossip about them.

_____ Belittle or use sarcasm.

_____ Hit physically.

_____ Manipulate into a "no win" situation.

_____ Try to control.

_____ Invade their boundaries.

17. When someone expresses anger toward me, I start feeling

_____ .

18. When you think about expressing anger directly at someone, what other feelings get stirred up within you? (For example, fear, anxiety, etc.)

_____ .

• What resistance messages to you give yourself when you think about expressing anger? (Example: "He probably won't like me if I show my anger.")

_____

_____ .

19. If you are married (or have been married) or have a roommate (or have had a roommate), remember the first time your spouse or roommate got angry with you.

• How did she/he express it? _____

_____ .

• When you got angry at him/her for the first time, how did you express it? _____

_____ .

20. Think of someone you're angry with. (Construct an "I feel" statement toward him/her. _____

_____

_____ .

• How do you feel while doing this?

_____

21. When you express anger toward another person, do you give an opportunity for that person to respond?_____.
    Do you actively *invite* the other person to respond?_____
22. Think about your life and actions during the past week:
    • How many times did you express your anger verbally appropriately?_____ inappropriately?_____
    • How did you feel afterward?   _____ .
    • How many times did you act it out?   _____ .
    • How did you feel afterward?   _____ .
23. Make a list of people toward whom you feel old anger. Make plans to share it with them or make plans to discharge it appropriately in some other way(s):

_____

_____

• Write a letter, then destroy it.
• Talk to the person, using the empty chair technique (place an empty chair in front of you, pretend you are talking to the person).
    • Talk to a therapist about it.
    • Pound an object, and label the object as that person.
    • Role-play (let another person sit in for that person).
    • Yell in the shower.
24. Integrating Your Anger
    A whole person is integrated and "invites" all parts of himself into his total being, even though he may not like (and even may feel repelled or horrified at some parts) each part.
    Draw a "floor plan" of your "house," identifying the occupants of the different "rooms." Label all the parts of yourself, such as: fears, joys, sexuality, spirituality, power, control, anger, etc. Which walls can you erase, symbolizing that you embrace that part of yourself into your whole? Which rooms are walled off because you are unable to accept that part of yourself?
25. Letting Your Anger Go

Create a visual picture of your anger.

Picture yourself letting it go in whatever way fits best with that image.

Write your personal philosophy about anger now that you have completed the inventory. _____

_____

_____

_____

4
Letting Go of the Judgment

The material in this chapter is based upon a series of lectures presented by John and Paula Sandford, who work in a field called *Inner Healing*.

Inner Healing

Ministers in Inner Healing pray with the client, pray for the client, and lead the client through a series of visualization exercises in which Christ comes into the person's memories and heals the wounds left by painful experiences. The minister also leads the client to visualize his or her parents and to forgive them for hurtful behavior, to ask their forgiveness for judging them, and to ask God's forgiveness for judging the parent.

Inner Wounds

Deep wounds can be inflicted upon a child's spirit while he or she is very young. The child forms judgments against his parents whenever he feels frustrated by the care he receives from them whether or not their behavior is hurtful. Of course, the child most certainly develops judgments when parents are abusive. In any case, the child's wounds need to be healed.

The child forms "bitter root judgments" against his parents because of those wounds. Made consciously or subsconsiously, they remain alive and active in the unconscious. Like roots, they lie beneath the surface, usually hidden.

In *The Transformation of the Inner Man,* John Sandford says:

Many pastors had little awareness of the formation of those practices (of forming bitter root judgments) in early childhood. They seemed to me like gardeners continually lopping off weeds which just as persistently regrew from the roots. None (pastors) seemed to comprehend the whole job, to lay the ax to the roots. They didn't seem to know how to transform our carnal natures at the deep level of *causes,* dealing both with sins and the sin nature. That, I saw, was the great lack in the Church, and therefore one explanation for the continued lack of maturity in the Body of Christ. Thus, many people were only patching old garments rather than slaying the old to replace the new.

Every sinful deed was fully washed away (at the New Birth), but . . . every part of the heart had not fully appropriated the good news of that fact. Many areas of the inner man have refused ever to lie down and accept that death.

So Christians proclaimed, "I'm born anew; the past is all gone," while the testimony of their lives all too often proclaimed the opposite.

A true and lasting change was not happening. Band-Aids were being applied to gaping wounds.

God's Universal Moral and Spiritual Laws

God built moral and spiritual laws into His universe, comparable to physical laws. The Ten Commandments contain those moral and spiritual laws in a condensed form. They reveal how reality operates according to God's design. The Ten Commandments work; our feelings do not affect their operation. God does not directly punish us when we break them; we reap in our body the results. "Men do shameful things with each other, and *as a result they bring upon themselves the punishment they deserve for their wrongdoing*" (Rom. 1:27, GNB, author's italics). When bad things happen, we are reaping the effects of law. God made one law to govern all people. He set in motion forces that will reap a result.

Leland, a thirty-year-old drug addict stepped out the window of a tenth-floor building. He lived but broke his body badly. Did God look down from on high and say, "I'm going to zap that young man because he used drugs"? No; the young man broke himself when he tested the law of gravity.

We have lost the awareness that everything in human relationships operates by the law of God. Our generation is aware of scientific laws and takes them seriously, yet we foolishly flout the most elementary moral and ethical laws. "For God hath not given us the spirit of fear; but of power, and of love, and of a sound mind" (2 Tim. 1:7). Why does God need to give us a sound mind? Because we do not have one—we are insane in a spiritual sense.

The Law of Sowing and Reaping

God set into the universe the Law of Judging and the Law of Sowing and Reaping. Hebrews 12:15 says, "Looking diligently lest any man fail of the grace of God; lest any root of bitterness springing up trouble you, and thereby many be defiled."

In Matthew 7:1-2 Jesus said: "Judge not, that ye be not judged. For with what judgment ye judge, ye shall be judged: and with what measure ye mete, it shall be measured to you again." Do not judge others, so that God will not judge you.

In Galatians 6:7 Paul said: "Do not deceive yourselves; no one makes a fool of God. A person will reap exactly what he plants" (GNB).

Paul told the Romans: "Do you, my friend, pass judgment on others? You have no excuse at all, whoever you are. For when you judge others and then do the same things which they do, you condemn yourself" (2:1, GNB).

In Colossians 3:9-10 Paul said, "Do not lie to one another, for you have put off the old self with its habits and have put on the new self" (GNB). Bitter roots are slain when we are converted, but sometimes we fail to show that the old self has been put aside.

When we judge, we condemn and blame; we hold anger and bitterness within our hearts toward the offender. One physical law states: For every action there is an equal and opposite reaction. The same is true within the moral and spiritual realm. God's law says: If you judge someone else of something, it dooms you to do same thing. When we judge, we reap the same behaviors within our own lives. Every formula must balance.

Judgment Against Parents

God's law says, "Honour thy father and thy mother: that thy days may be long upon the land which the Lord thy God giveth thee" (Ex. 20:12). We sow seed as children that we reap as adults. When parents treat a child abusively, bitter root judgments come as natural responses from the child. What happened with the parent is not as important as the fact that the child judged the parent. The wounds and angry feelings carried by the child infect the mind with negative psychological expectancies; as judgments, they necessitate reaping of seed sowed. The law is unchangeable. We need to dig out those roots that formed when we were very young.

Results of Judgment

Judgment comes back on us.—It sets us up us to repeat the same behaviors we judged. Many times a person said, "When I have children, I won't talk to them, hit them, or withdraw from them the way my parents did." That person, when a parent, feels horrified to see himself doing and hears himself saying the same hurtful things as his parents.

Judgment sets up expectations.—A bitter root expectancy (self-fulfilling prophecy, life script) is a psychological construct by which we expect life to go in a given way. We see life that way whether it is that way or not, and we draw those elements (events, people, experiences) to us. Bitter root judgments provoke responses, not merely by psychological weight of expectancy but by the power of law.

Judgment sets up two types of expectations:

(1) We draw into our lives the same types of people as those we judged. A woman vows, "I will never marry an alcoholic man like my father." She not only marries one but three in quick succession.

(2) We draw out of the people in our lives the same qualities and behaviors that exist in the people we judged. Our bitter roots can thereby defile, or at least adversely influence, others.

God wants to give us good things at all times but our expectations based upon our judgments block that giving.

Joyce, when five years old, lay in bed and heard her parents' loud voices downstairs. She got up and went to the head of the stairs. "Mommy and Daddy, what's wrong? Can I help?"

"Go back to bed!" the tense parents ordered her. The frightened child went back to bed.

The fighting continued each night. One night she heard a loud noise. Daddy had hit Mommy. Inside, the terrified girl screamed, "Daddy, I hate you! How can you treat my mother that way?"

She made a judgment against her dad: "I hate you."

As Joyce grew up, her father changed into a gentle, loving man and she forgot the judgment she made, but it stayed inside her. Judgment comes back whether the person remembers it or not.

Joyce married a young man who seemed to be congenial. One day she worked hard to clean the house and cook a special dinner for her husband. When he came in that night, the first thing she said was, "You've got mud all over your shoes! I've just mopped the floors and you're tracking in mud. And you're late, too! I've worked hard cooking your favorite meal, and you can't even come home on time."

He counterattacked. "I work hard all day—even work late—for you, and this is the thanks I get when I come home!"

The couple had their first fight. The conflict escalated until he hit her. What made a kind husband hit her? Admitting that he probably had problems of his own, it is also possible that her bitter root expectation that said, "Men will be violent," broadcasted to her husband, "Someday you're going to hit me."

Bitter Roots and Free Will

Where does her husband's free will operate in this exchange? we ask. Joyce's psychological expectation does not have the power to overcome his free will. Bitter-root judgments do not deny free will. The other person remains free not to respond to expectancy or law. But to do so, he must wade upstream against a torrent. Unless the grace of God intervenes, the person will eventually succumb to the pressure that comes from the expectation of the other.

We draw into our lives people whose judgments against their parents match ours. We almost always marry someone whose sowing and reaping fits ours. When we marry, we reap what the partner has judged. When a couple marries, the question is, "Will my mate get better with me or worse? Will she/he drink from my strengths and overcome his/her weaknesses, or will the opposite take place?" In Joyce's case, for example, she probably drew out her husband's own bitter root judgments of his parents. Consider another case.

Bert grew up with a heavy, slovenly mother who was a poor housekeeper. He hated that and he made this judgment: "Women are heavy and they will mess up my house and my life."

His slender wife, Marcia, had a critical father. She made this judgment: "The man will be critical."

When Marcia got pregnant, she gained weight. After the birth of the baby, it was hard for her to get rid of the extra pounds. Bert felt angry and started criticizing her. Marcia then felt insecure, ate more, and got heavier. Bert critized more and the cycle continued. His wife felt badly about herself and stopped taking care of her personal grooming and the housework. She became just like his mother. Bert reaped the judgment he made years earlier.

With John Sandford's help, Bert forgave his mother and asked God to remove the judgment and to give him a new heart that would expect a slim wife. Bert's wife forgave her father and asked God to take her sin to the cross and asked Him to give her a new expectation that the man would not be critical. By working through past judgments, the couple developed realistic expectations for each other.

John Sandford grew up on a ranch in Oklahoma. His mother—a typical ranch woman—restrained her emotions and did not praise or show affection to her son. Mother valued people by how much they could work. She made John work long hours, criticized him, and withheld praise. He judged her and formed this expectation: "The woman will make me work long hours; I won't get praise or affection and I will get criticized."

His wife, Paula, judged her parents for being critical. Her father traveled as a salesman and stayed away from home three weeks at a time. Paula loved him. On the Friday evening he was due to come home, little Paula sat by the front window, watching anxiously. He did not actually come late, but her impatience made her form a judgment: "Daddy is late. He is gone when I need him. He isn't here for me." She unknowingly set up this expectation: "The man will be late."

After John and Paula got married, he developed a problem with promptness, one he had never had before. When Paula recognized her criticisms resulted from her judgment on her father, John's habits regarding time improved.

John worked hard for his wife and thought that would bring praise from her, but it brought criticism. Her judgment of her father and his of his mother converged to produce a very unhappy situation.

When the couple first married, Paula gave John a lot of affection. He pushed her away, although inwardly he loved it. After a few years, Paula stopped showing affection. He had reaped the judgment he made against his mother. When he realized that his early judgment that he would never receive affection was causing him to push his wife aside, Paula's naturally affectionate nature sprang forth again.

John's mother cleaned house inconsistently. At times, she cleaned perfectly; at times, the house looked like a wreck. John's expectation: "The woman will be a poor housekeeper."

Paula's expectations played into John's. Her parents would go out and leave her, the oldest child, in charge of the household. She would clean and her four younger brothers would demolish her work. Her judgment: "Boys mess up my housecleaning."

After she got married, she cleaned and her sons messed up. John criticized her; she felt tense; the children picked up on that tension and did what she expected them to do. She reaped her judgment, and it meshed with her husband's.

When both recognized the cause of their critical nature and put away judgments, things changed. Almost overnight, Paula transformed into an efficient housekeeper. "Our house is now Grand Central Station," John says, "but Paula keeps it in order."

Paula also judged her brothers because she felt embarrassed when they behaved rambunctiously at school. After she married John, he—a young minister—began to make embarrassing slips of the tongue from the pulpit. On the drive to church each Sunday morning, she said, "You're not going to say anything to embarrass me today, are you?" John noticed that when Paula was not present, he did not say that type of thing. When Paula dealt with her feelings about her brothers and stopped "expecting" her husband to say something embarrassing, John's propensity toward verbal slips stopped.

Reaping Judgments in Work Settings

A man named Edward grew up with an alcoholic gambling father who put his son to work at age eleven. If the father (who did not work) found the money the son earned, he stole it and spent it on liquor and gambling. Edward judged his father for his actions. He set up an expectation: "Men will steal from me and mess up my life."

When grown, Edward started a business. Every partner he ever had lied, didn't work, and stole from him. One even seduced his wife. Edward sought a church deacon as a partner, considering him to be trustworthy. When Edward was hospitalized, the partner tried to have him declared incompetent so the deacon could steal the business.

Edward worked through his judgment against his father. Within a few weeks, all the dishonest men in his company were replaced with solid workers. Edward got a loan from the bank. In the past the bank had turned down his loan requests because of the previous employees.

Mitchell's father was a pastor who gave some much away that his family suffered. He judged his father and God: God the Father will give away everything to others. I will have nothing.

When Mitchell became a pastor, his expectations were fulfilled. Though his church was large, his income was so low that he had to drive a bus to make ends meet. Members he trained well moved to other churches. From Mitchell's perspective, God the Father was continuing the old pattern of taking from Mitchell to give to others.

Finally, Mitchell saw that the problem lay in his judgment of his father and its resultant expectations. When he put the judgment behind him, the pattern began to change and the situation improved.

Letting Go of the Judgments

In childhood, we sow that which in time we shall reap. If we are ever to be freed from the cycle, we must do three things. First, forgive our parents for any hurtful behavior. Second, ask our parents to forgive us for judging them. (This can be done by use of visualization, role-play, etc.) Finally, ask God to forgive us for judging our parents. *This process cuts us free and stops those judgments and expectancies from acting out in our lives.*

John Sandford says that the primary need for most of his clients is to be set free from their bitter root judgments and expectancies.

I have been through this process myself with trained counselors, and it was one of the most cleansing, most liberating experiences in my spiritual development. I saw with new eyes what I had done by judging my parents and saw how those judgments have played themselves out in my life. I gained a new awareness of the awfulness of judging and found that the habit was so deeply ingrained in my life that it was a reflexive action, one that I must renounce daily. I now incorporate this concept in my counseling and refer my clients to those trained in this field.

Donald, 60, read this chapter and asked: "How does this fit for a person like me? It was progress for me to acknowledge that I felt angry at my parents because I had felt that was a sin. You, as a counselor, know how important it is for a person to get in touch with his feelings. This material stirs up my guilts and makes me feel, at least temporarily, that I must not feel angry toward my parents."

Children make judgments against their parents before they are old enough to make any conscious choice about behavior. It is important for all of us to claim our inner feelings. For Donald to deny or suppress his genuine angry feelings toward his parents would not kid his inner self or God—he knows and God knows he felt angry. He needs to renounce the judgments rather than feel guilty about his feelings of anger.

When I turned loose the judgments against my parents, it was then that I could see them through the eyes of compassion. The process did not stir up my feelings of guilt; the process helped me to turn loose those angry feelings that I had previously acknowledged.

Activities

Write in this book or use a separate notebook.

1. Write judgments you have made against your father.
   Example: I judged him for being a drunk.

_____

_____

_____

_____

_____

_____

_____ .

2. Write judgments you have made against your mother.
   Example: I judged her for staying with my father and not
leaving.

_____

_____

_____

_____

_____ .

3. Write judgments you made against brothers.
   Example: I judged him for criticizing me constantly.

_____

_____

_____

_____ .

4. Write judgments you made against sisters.
   Example: I judged her for bossing me.

_____

_____

_____

_____ .

Go through the same process for in-laws, spouses, or anyone against whom you have formed judgments.

When you feel able to let go of the judgments, you can do so. As with forgiveness, this experience is not a formula where you snap your fingers and make things go away. When, in the depths of your heart, you are ready to let go, do so, but the pain and anger need to be worked through. You need a minister or counselor trained in this field to lead you through this process.

Forgiveness Takes Time

A critically injured young man was admitted to the emergency room of a hospital. He had received severe cuts in an automobile accident. A surgeon sewed up the visible cuts, but the patient bled to death seven hours later. The surgeon had not sewed up a cut artery that was not visible on the surface. The physician sewed the skin together so that everything looked all right on the surface, but death lurked inside.

Forgiveness does not come cheaply with little stitches here and there. Religious people, especially, tend to handle their guilt by rushing through to forgiveness before they take care of the inner work. John Sandford said, "Counselors shouldn't be in such a rush to make people well!" It was the process of which he spoke. No two people's timetable is identical.

Another question arises in this area that is comparable to the forgiveness issue: Must I do this work in person with my parent?

This is primarily inner work for you. If you went to a parent and said, "I no longer judge you for beating me," that could come across as a judgment!

A young woman asked me: "What can I do about my father? I have forgiven him for his beating me, but when I tell him that, he denies that he ever beat me! I keep on after him trying to get him to admit that it took place."

Talking to a parent may not be the important thing; cleaning out your own spiritual and emotional closet is what is necessary.

5
Boundary Issues

"An important developmental task of a child involves discovery and establishment of one's own boundaries, and recognition of the boundaries of others," says Sharon I. Eve.

We need boundaries for two reasons: They help us define ourselves as separate and different from others, and they help us connect with others.

Definition of Boundaries

I use a tale of five fences as an analogy to describe boundaries and their function. Individuals may operate out of more than one of these boundary styles at different times. Let's say that we take a leisurely drive through a rural area on a Sunday afternoon. First we come to an open field with no fences. Would the owner put cows in that field? Hardly. The cows would wander off, get lost, or be hit by motor vehicles. Someone could steal the cows by entering the unprotected space.

This field without fences would be similar to individuals and/or families who have *lost or nonexistent boundaries.* Bradshaw compares a person without boundaries to a country without borders or a house without doors. Incest victims, for example, have no sense of boundaries.

Sandy grew up in a home with an alcoholic father. Her two older brothers had sex with her. When she dated as an adult, if she liked the young man well enough to invite him inside the front door at the end of the evening, she had sex with him automatically without discrimination. If she didn't like him well enough for him to come in, she didn't have sex. She has done important work in her own recovery and that does not happen any more.

Next, we come to a field containing cows but the fence is broken at places. The cows can get out; predators can come in. The cows are not protected. The fence presents a confused picture: Does the owner expect the cows to stay in or not? This compares to individuals and/or families with *unclear boundaries.*

Unclear boundaries can take place in the work setting as well as in families. "Two young people are working for me today, so I have to go back to the office after this appointment," Evan said, as he met me one Saturday morning for his regular appointment. "At least, I think they're working for me," he laughed. "When I tell them to do something, they do it, but I never have understood who their supervisor is. Nobody ever told me."

The third field has a strong fence as it faces the road but the fence that borders the neighboring field is entangled with the neighbor's fence. We cannot tell where one property ends and the other begins. Farmer A's cows can wander into Farmer B's field and vice versa. This would show *enmeshed* or blurred or diffuse boundaries. In these families, members focus on fitting together at the expense of the separate identity of each person. Enabling behavior, or taking care of others, results.

Connie needs to move to another state with her new husband. Her joy over her personal situation is overshadowed by her concern about her daughter and grandchild. "I'm feeling so desperate because I don't have time to make arrangements for my daughter before I leave. She doesn't have a job, and I'm feeling as if I'm abandoning her if I just walk off."

Connie needs to distance herself from her daughter. The mother has taken on the younger woman's problems as if they were her own.

A pastor of a distant church called me and asked if I could drive an unemployed woman to a job interview near me. When I called the woman, I learned that she was divorced and had an eight-year-old daughter. When I told her I could not go at the time she needed to go, she "got huffy" and hung up on me.

A day later, I called back and the child answered. She put her hand over the phone and said to her mother, "It's Mrs. Martin; do you want me to tell her you're not at home?" That mother and daughter had severely enmeshed boundaries.

As we continue our drive through the countryside, we come to a tall, thick brick wall that we assume hides an estate from view. We cannot see the house and the occupants cannot see out. This would compare to *rigid* boundaries. Sometimes individuals and/or families develop rigid boundaries that keep them locked inside and prevent anyone else from coming in.

Sometimes people use rigid boundaries to protect themselves, so rigid boundaries can be important for survival. Children may retreat from the family having learned that contact means discomfort or pain. They may fear that they will lose *self* and be engulfed by the parents and/or the family dynamics. A fear of rejection can cause a person to build rigid boundaries. This person eventually feels alone and isolated.

Harriet, forty-nine, says, "I really worry about my forty-four-year-old brother. Three wives have divorced him, and he never sees his three children who live in another state. He goes to work and then retreats into his house. The only time I see him is when I contact him."

The last field we see on our trip has a barbed wire fence in good condition. We see the cows in the pasture, but they cannot get out. This correlates with clear, *permeable* boundaries. Healthy boundaries protect the person, but he can see out and others can see in. The person chooses when to invite someone into his private space and chooses when to come out to enter someone else's space.

When the boundary within the family is clear and permeable, individuals retain their unique individuality. These people can talk to each other assertively, rather than aggressively or avoid each other (passivity). They can take risks; they develop ways to resolve conflicts and power struggles; they can be flexible; and they know how to set clearly defined limits. They are willing to be open and visible to one another in contrast to the minimal visibility adopted by a child in the alcoholic home.

People who have healthy boundaries can say no and know when

and how to say it appropriately. Recently, one of my grown daughters said, "The Academy Theater in Atlanta called and asked me to give them ninety dollars over the next twelve months." I felt annoyed because her finances are so tight that we help her. (Take note of the enmeshment!) So, essentially, it is our money she agreed to give because she has no extra. That theater can hardly be viewed as a needy organization. I would have felt differently if the request came from a hungry family. (She canceled her pledge.) As I thought about the situation, I realized that my husband and I have not modeled for her how one says no.

Shortly after my minister husband and I got married, I invited my friend Jackie to spend a week with us helping with Vacation Bible School. One afternoon a church member whom I'll call Mrs. Burton called while my husband and I were taking a nap. Jackie took the call and told Mrs. Burton that we were asleep and could return the call later. Mrs. Burton insisted—demanded—that Jackie wake one of us even though the matter was not urgent.

The next day Mrs. Burton's friend, whom I'll call Mrs. Walters, came up to me and reported the incident in this manner: Jackie had done something very wrong not to wake us; she and Mrs. Burton both felt very angry toward Jackie, and they assumed that we, too, would feel angry toward her.

The church members had never heard us say no to any request before, so Mrs. Burton reacted with anger the first time a no came from our home.

A few years later, a couple spent the week in our home while their daughter got medical help in that area. At the end of their stay, they said, "We have never in our lives heard people say 'yes' so totally to others. We have not heard you say 'no' to any church member who called this week."

My husband and I had a poor sense of personal boundaries, and this is what our daughters learned from us. Shortly after the call from the theater, that daughter was in our home when I got a call from a genuinely needy situation in our county. I said, "I am already overextended in my benevolent efforts so I cannot contribute now."

"That was nicely said," my daughter commented. When she observes us saying no in a courteous way, she may learn how to do the same thing.

Privacy and Boundaries

Sometimes people feel confused about the difference between intimacy and invasion of boundaries. Partners in a healthy relationship try to tell each other what their boundaries are, since people vary greatly in their need for privacy. People need to have their space respected if they are to function at their best. People get confused about the difference between boundaries and barriers. Barriers say: "Keep out." Boundaries say: "Come in at my request." A boundary says: "Stay out right now." A barrier says: "Stay out forever."

Boundary disorders served a need for the child when situations seemed life-threatening. When adults carry these patterns over into present-day relationships, those disorders block development of relationships that are solid and mutually satisfying. Experiences that seemed life threatening then are only scary now.

Withdrawing/Contacting Others

Mature people have a healthy contact/withdrawal pattern with the world around them. They keep a balance with their environment—they do not withdraw completely, neither do they allow their environment to envelop them. They do not become a victim of others, neither do they dominate them. They have a rhythm of contact and withdrawing. This rhythm meets a person's needs.

"In a dysfunctional home, this rhythm is usually out of order," say Maureen T. and Jeremiah P. Bresnahan. "So family members often resort to controlling, manipulating, enabling, withdrawing from, adjusting to, and distracting other family members in order to get their needs met. The Adult Children bring these patterns of contact into adulthood and future relationships unless they receive help."

Adult Children usually behave in extremes when this contact/withdrawing rhythm is out of balance. The Bresnahans say, "Overcontacting the environment leads to boredom, stagnation, insomnia, and anxiety; while overwithdrawing results in daydreaming, oversleeping, loneliness, mental disorders, and often alcoholism."

These adults feel confused and ask themselves these questions:
- When should I reach out and when should I draw back?
- When should I speak and when should I stay quiet?
- What is appropriate and what is inappropriate?
- What is real and what is fantasy?
- When should I say yes and when should I say no?

Adult Children find it hard to identify the primary need, have trouble making a decision, and usually wind up unhappy and confused when they make decisions. The contact and the withdrawal are not effective, so they wind up feeling uncomfortable with themselves and dissatisfied in relationships with others.

The Bresnahans describe five personality types that children of alcoholics show as they act out the boundary distances that interfere with contacting the environment in a healthy way. The *Introjector* acts like a blotter, absorbing the rules, values, and standards of behavior other people lay out for him. He uses them for his own without making any choice. As a child, he thought safety lay in obeying the rules. As an adult, he cannot do what he wants because he has no experience either in knowing what he wants or in doing what he wants. He feels little enthusiasm for life and often becomes depressed, develops psychosomatic illnesses, and/or marries an alcoholic (workaholic, physical abuser, etc.). He gives in to fit in. He is a passive placater who waits for others to give him permission to live.

Winston is a good attorney. But he doesn't want to be an attorney—this was the career Dad chose for Winston, who didn't have the courage to take his own stand. His periods of depression are coming more frequently.

An Introjector lives by clichés and slogans he heard as a child. A fellow worker of mine usually had a slogan to fit every occasion when she faced conflict. "A word to the wise is sufficient," and so forth.

The *Projector* blames others for what actually begins in her. She projects her unacceptable thoughts or feelings onto others. Thus, she becomes a victim of circumstances. For instance, she might change her unacceptable anger toward an abusive parent into a belief that the parent hated her.

The Projector has a lot of paranoia. She accuses other people of being unfriendly, "out to get you," and so forth. She does not realize that her main goal is to keep separate and alienated from others. Therefore, she says that others are abusing her (which justifies staying away from them).

A male fellow worker of mine was "Quick-Draw McGraw" when it came to attacking others. "You gave me the wrong directions!" he typically accused peers. When asked how he got lost in the city, he would say, "When I got to the place where you said to turn right, that didn't look correct, so I turned left instead," or "When I got to a certain landmark, that seemed too far so I turned around and came back." He never apologized for the unfair blame nor did he learn from the experience that it was he who bungled. That type of incident reoccurred, and he continued to see himself as a victim.

The *Reflector* withdraws from the family (and later, the broader society), concluding that he cannot depend on anyone. He becomes self-sufficient. He is not in touch with his feelings.

"I never get angry," Phil says. "It never did any good when I was a child, so now I don't bother." His anger is there, of course, but he is not in touch with it.

"The Reflector turns his aggressions inward and drives or punishes himself," say the Bresnahans. "These held-in emotions make him prone to physical ailments, such as heart attacks, ulcers, arthritis, eating disorders, and high blood pressure." He may grind his teeth, trying to hold feelings in. He is afraid that he will be hurt and will hurt others so he rarely takes risks.

The *Confluencer* merges his identity with those around him. It is important to him that everyone be alike. This is the "perfect child" who had too much responsibility. He feels anxious when he tries to break away as a young adult. He may be able to move away physically but remains chained to his family emotionally.

Charlotte, twenty-five, lives in a Western state. Her father is in the military and her parents live in another country. Whenever she needs to make a decision, even a trivial one, she calls her parents and asks them to tell her what to do. "I wish she could make her own decisions, right or wrong," her mother says.

"The *Confluencer*," the Bresnahans say, is usually a slave to tradition, habit, and routine. He gives unwanted advice freely, and always knows the best way—his way. He tends to be compulsive and frequently experiences anxiety when an alternative course of action is used. He is too dependent on others for his identity and happiness, and when people don't conform to his wishes, he becomes anxious and resentful. He tends to "cling" to people, places, and things and to hang on to the past.

The *Deflector* is the clown, the joker, the one who diverts when things get too hot. Afraid of intimacy, he keeps everything at a surface level. He denies what is happening in the family and believes that magically every problem will go away.

Importance of Boundaries

Bradshaw says that one of our basic needs is structure and that we ensure our structure by developing a boundary system.

A person who has no boundaries has no limits and can easily get confused. She can go in this direction and that, wasting much energy and getting lost. This inability to set limits leads people to become addicted because they don't know when to stop and how to say no. Effective boundaries are important for children and adults.

How Children Develop Boundaries

Parents model boundaries before their children. When the parents have a clear sense of their own boundaries, they exhibit independence and autonomy as individuals and in relationship to their spouses and children. These parents have their own values and have clear agendas for their lives. They take responsibility for their lives rather than cling to spouses, children, and others. They do not blame others for any shortcomings or disappointments in their situations. They respect "differentness" in a spouse and children, and differences in viewpoint, feelings, and behavior would be accepted.

Parents give children permission to have boundaries. These parents feel comfortable when children show signs of individuating. If a young child expresses anger toward the parents, they do not take it personally but hear it as an expression of the child's legitimate feelings. These parents set limits on *how* negative feelings are expressed rather than deny that expression or try to make the children feel guilty for expressing negative feelings.

A mother of a newborn son said, "I can't wait until he is old enough to put his arms around my neck and say, 'Mommy, I love you.' "

"He will also say, 'I hate you!' one day," I told her.

Her eyes widened. "Why do you say that?"

"Because you said it to your mother, didn't you?"

She nodded thoughtfully. "Yes, I did."

It is typical for young children at times to yell, "I hate you!" to a parent and to even hit the parent.

The parent could say, "I see that you're feeling angry at me. You may not hit me, but I would be glad for you to talk to me about how you're feeling." It would also help if the parent knew that underneath the anger lies other feelings, perhaps hurt, frustration, and/or jealousy. Often "I hate you!" follows setting a limit that frustrates the child. It is important that the child be able to talk about how he feels but that the parent remain firm about the limits.

When one of my young children showed anger toward me, and we began talking about her feelings, I often shifted into an indulgent mood. Then I usually lifted the limit because that closeness with the child felt so good I didn't want to threaten it by remaining firm. Now I know that holding to limits is important for the child's security.

The teen years turn out to be turbulent for many families because that is the stage when children normally start separating from the parents. When they feel threatened and uncomfortable, when children disagree with their viewpoints, criticize their behavior, and want to do things differently, parents control, attack, and in other ways resist this normal process. Parents who respect boundaries expect teens to begin to move away from the family. Those who receive permission from parents to make that break healthily will come back later. Those who must rebel in a hostile way to achieve separateness may not return or they may remain in a combative state for years.

Parents interact with children in a way that gives children practice in developing boundaries. Mother could say, "I understand that you don't want me to go out right now, but I have an appointment and

I must go." She could encourage the child to talk about his feelings, but she would not reorder her life because of the child's objection.

Parents could say, "I'm feeling angry with you right now because of what you did." Children could see that it is OK to feel angry at people we love and could see the parent modeling how to handle anger constructively.

The child's wishes would be considered in making family decisions, such as where to eat, where to go for recreational outings, rather than the parents making autocratic decisions.

The children could see the parents work through differences of opinion and wishes.

How Children's Boundaries Are Violated

Daily life brings about numerous situations in which boundaries may be violated. Parents may be careless about locking doors while having sex, and children may walk in and observe parents having sex. On the other hand, parents can violate children's boundaries if they do not observe children's closed doors and allow children no privacy. Children need to be taught to lock their doors or be given permission to lock their doors. Parents sometimes walk into the bathroom or bedroom when children are nude. This violates a boundary. Likewise, parents need to be dressed in front of children. That helps set sexual boundaries.

Children need to have privacy in general, not only when dressing. Parents should not eavesdrop on phone conversations or read diaries or letters. Ideally each child has his own room where he can have private space. This may not be possible but, when a child is in his room, he needs to be free to close the door unless the parent knows or suspects strongly that the child is doing something dangerous or destructive or specifically forbidden.

Rules about doors show up in dysfunctional families. In one home where incest took place, the father made the rule that no one could ever close a bedroom door.

Janet experienced no overt sexual or physical abuse, but her father coached her two older brothers to tease her persistently and without mercy. They took her door off so she could never retreat and protect herself from the boundary violations. They came in while she was sleeping and tickled her, squirted things into her mouth, etc. If she ever protested, the others said, "We're just having fun. You're no fun. You have a bad attitude." At fourteen, Janet developed a bleeding ulcer. The parents said to the physician, "We can't imagine what stress she might be under because we have fun all day at home."

Sometimes a mother uses enemas to force the child's toilet training. That is a violation of the child's body boundary. For his healthy development, he needs to choose to release the stool rather than have it forced according to the desire and convenience of the adult. Toilet training in that manner can lead to sexual dysfunctioning.

Adults and Personal Boundaries

Adults also may have difficulty setting and maintaining boundaries. Wayne, forty-nine, recognizes that he has weak personal boundaries. What can he do now?

- Counseling can give guidance and support to an adult attempting to establish boundaries.

- Adults can learn about the concepts of boundaries and give themselves permission to develop boundaries—emotional, physical, social, and spiritual.

- Adults can take assertiveness training classes and practice setting limits and claiming their space with others. Claiming one's space often involves parents. It can mean that the adult will move away from his parents. One's residence defines one's borders. When grown children remain at home, it can be an indication of enmeshed boundaries. In many cases the grown child and the parents can be friends as long as they live separately, and see each other by choice, whereas living under the same roof causes constant friction.

A thirty-year-old single woman wrote Ann Landers saying that her mother wanted a key to the daughter's apartment, so she complied. One night, the mother entered the apartment after the daughter was asleep. The daughter thought an intruder was breaking in. "It scared me to death!" she wrote. She feared that her mother might walk in and interrupt a romantic moment when the daughter had a date. "What can I do?" she asked Ann.

Ann Landers recommended that the young woman tell Mother her fears about Mother coming in during the night. The daughter might consider changing locks and keeping a key for herself only. Mother was invading the boundaries of her daughter. A grown child (single or married) needs to retain control over when parents visit. Parents need to call first (or write if they live a distance away) and get clearance to come over. The same would be true for adult brothers and sisters and friends.

On an "Oprah Winfrey Show," four mothers appeared with their grown, married daughters who were themselves mothers. Each grandmother was trying to control how her daughter raised her children. Some tried to persuade; some criticized and gave unasked-for advice. One grandmother said, "My daughter and I argue about this on the phone sometimes three times a day." One grandmother told that she instructed her daughter (in her thirties) to get off the phone and punish the child who was interrupting on the other phone.

One grandmother had a syrupy, sweet style. "I just want my daughter to raise her child the way I raised mine."

Another grandmother had a dogmatic style. "My daughter ought to spank more often! That's a lot quicker than all this 'talking to' she does with her son. She ought to take care of things and be done with it."

At no point did a mother, daughter, Oprah, or the visiting psychologist address the fundamental issue: These mothers were invading the boundaries of their daughters in trying to impose their viewpoints on parenting. Each woman still held onto her daughter rather than releasing her to be an individual and to be free to choose her own style of parenting. Each woman was saying, in effect, "I want my daughter to be like me and to do what I would do." The mothers' positions were disrespectful of their daughters' rights to be individuals. Each mother was invading the home of another person (and her husband) and was interfering with her daughter's maturing process. The daughters in these instances cannot develop confidence as individuals or as parents as long as their mothers are hovering in the wings saying constantly, "You're doing it wrong. Do it my way."

These mothers and daughters were battling a foundational issue by focusing on surface matters. The basic question is: Does my daughter have the right to be an independent person and conduct her life in her manner even if it differs from mine?

A secondary issue was one of trust. No mother said, or implied, "I trust my daughter to do a good job raising her child." Inquiry from Oprah revealed that no daughter was abusing her child. The arguments dealt with topics such as the age of toilet-training and how much time a child watched TV. Unless a grown child is abusing a child, a grandparent should respect boundaries and keep his or her fingers out of the situation.

Sometimes the grown child invades boundaries of the parents. Wayne is learning about and practicing boundaries. One of his daughters has an eating disorder that sounds like anorexia. She eats very little because she is obsessed with staying thin. "I used to try to make her eat," he says. "Now I know that I cannot control her. I work on my relationship with her in general and do not make comments about her eating any more."

The daughter attends a university on the other side of town, and it seems to Wayne that she clings excessively to her parents. She shows this by calling several times a day. Wayne bought an answering machine so he can have more choice about when he talks with his daughter. He also does not want to reinforce her habit of "running home to parents" for even the smallest problem. "If we are always available, she has no opportunity to learn that she can cope on her own," he concludes.

Sometimes both parents are at home when their daughter calls and leaves a message. Wayne says, "I'm not available now. I'll call her later."

His wife argues, "I think we should pick up the phone the minute she calls," which indicates that the mother has enmeshed boundaries with her daughter. It is hard for her to tolerate her daughter's feelings of frustration when she doesn't get an immediate response from her parents.

Boundary Problems at Work

The workplace offers many challenges for adults who have difficulty with boundaries. John Neikirk says: "Boundary problems will show up in Adult Children as compulsive work behavior. They will have trouble delegating to others, feeling they have to do all the work themselves because no one else could do it as well. They over-or-under manage their subordinates, have trouble working as a team player (their old manipulative family survival roles resurface), and tend to have very unrealistic expectations of their boss, subordinates and clients . . . not to mention themselves."

William, over the years, has had problems getting his work done. "I was always running around finding out what was going on in other departments," he said. Now he makes a contract with himself each morning as he drives to work: "I will complete the tasks I have to do and will stay at my desk." He noticed that he got more work done whenever he went into work sick—he didn't feel like running all over the place!

As adults develop a sense of boundaries, they don't start calling friends and monopolizing their time. Shirley made "mother figures" out of women friends. When she felt needy, she would call another woman and keep her on the line an hour without checking out the other's availability or willingness. Or she would drop in on a friend unannounced and "dump on her" for an hour. Now, Shirley asks, "Do you have a few minutes? Is this a convenient time to talk?" and makes advance appointments to see friends. This means that sometimes she must "sit on her feelings," rather than find an immediate outlet, but she feels better about herself and no longer alienates others through inappropriate self-disclosing.

How Adults' Boundaries Are Violated

These are ways that people invade others' boundaries:
- Sexual abuse,
- Physical abuse,
- Rape,
- Asking personal questions.

• Asking another to explain one's actions or viewpoint—calling on the other to justify oneself to the inquirer.

• Giving unasked-for advice—telling someone else how to live his/her life, in general.

• Telling another what one thinks of the other's behavior when it does not affect the speaker. (For example, criticizing how the other person dresses.)

• Listening to phone conversations.

• Reading diaries, letters, etc.

• Telling another what God wants that person to do.

• Repeating confidential material whether the hearer promised confidentiality or not, but especially when confidentiality was pledged.

• Entering a bedroom and/or bathroom without knocking.

• Committing someone to do something without first securing that person's agreement.

• Dropping in for a visit unannounced.

• Lingering too long on a phone visit or when a guest, ignoring signals from the other person.

• Trying to force one's viewpoint on another or showing disrespect for another's viewpoint.

• Using another's clothing or property without permission.

• Trying to force grown children to live according to parents' desires and/or values.

• Person A telling person B's business to person C.

• Intruding at a gathering, such as joining others at a restaurant without being invited.

• Moving in to live with another, or with parents, without permission.

• Pursuing another person when she/he has given adequate signals that she/he has ended the relationship—romantic, friendly, or otherwise.

• Taking charge of children when their parents are present, such as correcting the children. (If they are doing something destructive, it is the parents to whom one should speak rather than deal with the children.

• Sharing personal information about oneself without checking out if the hearer wants to hear it.

• By inappropriate touch: in places the person doesn't want to be touched; at times the person doesn't want to be touched; in a manner the person doesn't want to be touched (includes hitting, sexual handling, tickling).

• Asking excessive or inappropriate favors.

• Telling another's story for him (especially if he doesn't want it told).

• Calling another by first name (when the relationship does not call for that).

• Breaking in line in front of another.

• Helping someone without checking first to see if he/she wants help.

• Making demands rather than requests.

• Pushing past another's "no" or any setting of limits.

• Interrupting another while talking

• Smoking in front of others without securing permission.

• Placing expectations on another without securing the other's agreement. For example: expecting a mother or father, husband or wife, boy or girl to perform certain duties because of sexual identity.

• Not cleaning up after oneself.

• Wearing another's clothes or using any property without permission.

• Disregarding time agreements, such as being late or early; pressuring a person to be ready earlier.

• Not returning, or being slow to return, borrowed items.

• Assumption of feelings—thinking we know what another feels or wants and perhaps taking action based on those assumptions without checking them out.

• Being "honest" in a hostile way that justifies and covers up hostility.

• Analyzing another person: telling another what he feels, why he feels as he does, or how he should or should not feel.

• Treating another person in a patronizing or condescending manner.

- Judging another.
- Expecting a return for a favor done.
- Indulging ourselves at the expense of another
- Creating triangles (trying to control one person through another).
- Using abusive language.
- Gossiping.

Setting Personal Boundaries

Those of us who grew up in rural areas heard the saying, "Good fences make good neighbors." Boundaries serve the same function as fences; good boundaries clarify, enhance, and smooth relationships between people. The following activities will help you clarify your boundary styles and begin setting appropriate boundaries.

Activities

Write in this book or use a separate notebook.
1. Which boundary style describes you?
   Nonexistent?
   Unclear?
   Enmeshed?
   Rigid?
   Clear, permeable?
2. What style describes the boundaries in your family of origin?

_____

3. If you are a parent, describe the boundary style of your present family.

_____

4. How many of the behaviors found in a family with clear boundaries do you exhibit?
   - Able to speak assertively?
   - Able to take risks?
   - Able to resolve conflicts/power struggles constructively?
   - Able to set clearly defined limits?
   - Able to be open and visible to others important to you?
   - Able to say no?
5. How would evaluate your withdrawing/contacting rhythm with your environment?
   - Do you overcontact?
   - Do you withdraw too much?
   - Do you have a balance?
6. Which personality type describes you best?
   - Introjector
   - Projector
   - Reflector
   - Confluencer
   - Deflector

Do you identify one of the above styles as a predominant style and another as a back-up style? For example, many people behave from a different style when under stress. It is possible that you identify yourself as belonging to two categories.

7. If you are married, what boundary issues exist between you and your spouse?

_____

_____

_____

_____

Are you able to talk to your spouse in a person-to-person, non-threatening way to work on resolving boundary violations?

8. If you are a parent, what boundary violations exist between you and the children, between you and your spouse and the children?

Describe action plans to move toward creating healthier boundaries.

_____

_____

_____

_____

_____

9. In what ways do you violate boundaries with peers and members of your family of origin?

_____

_____

_____

_____

10. Describe action plans to correct the above violations.

_____

_____

_____

_____

11. In what ways does it seem to you that other people violate your boundaries?

_____

_____

_____

_____

12. Are you able to talk to those individuals, express your feelings and request new behaviors from them?

Example: "I need to talk to you about something important. When you do _____, I feel _____. I want to ask you to do _____ instead."

13. What boundary problems exist for you in the work setting?

_____

_____

_____

_____

14. Describe action plans for clarifying those issues.

_____

_____

_____

_____

6
Trust Issues

Alcoholic and co-dependent parents serve as poor role models for openness and trust in relationships. The alcoholic atmosphere contains deceit, secrecy, and unkept promises. It is natural for Adult Children to have difficulty in forming close, trusting, and secure relationships.

Gayle Rosellini and Mark Worden say, "The hidden reservoir of distrust, disillusionment and hurt feelings we hold inside from the alcoholic home poisons a current intimate relationship.

"A person may feel so hurt, so burned by life, that he is no longer willing to reach out for love and intimacy."

When we cannot trust:
We become fearful and anxious.
We try to control.
We develop feelings of paranoia.
We become paralyzed, unable to take action.
We become closed and self-protective rather than open.
We withhold rather than give.
We build walls rather than bridges, isolating ourselves from others and God.
We assume the worst about others rather than the best.
We believe others and God do not care and become self-pitying.
Thinking we carry the load alone, we feel overwhelmed.
We become pessimistic rather than optimistic.
We use our emotional and spiritual energies destructively rather than constructively.
We live unbalanced lives.

We make unwise choices and hasty decisions; we behave impulsively.

We lose our spontaneity and ability to play.

We feel hopeless and become discouraged.

We become stagnant and block the flow of our lives.

We become greedy rather than generous.

We discount our feelings.

We narrow our focus.

We become hostile.

We give up our option of choice—to choose to trust.

We lose ground in our recovery rather than move forward.

We develop tensions that affect our physical health.

We become cynical, even jaded.

We conflict with others.

We leap to conclusions.

We head in too many directions at once.

We become critical and judgmental.

We become jealous and envious.

We react rather than act; we overreact and panic.

We set up negative self-fulfilling prophecies.

We become rigid rather than flexible.

We stop dreaming and focus obsessively on the present dilemma.

We start projecting our own fears and anxieties onto others.

We go around in circles, depleting our energies and repeating mistakes.

We feel lonely.

We give away the control of our lives to other people and to circumstances.

We feel confused.

We doubt our own feelings and abilities to cope.

We abandon ourselves by blocking our own progress rather than aiding it and by making decisions that hurt us.

We make assumptions about others rather than check things out.

We try to manipulate and use others.

We become intolerant and limited in our acceptance of others.

We view the world as hostile and ungiving.

We take a short view rather than a long view.

We think things will never change.

We get into delusion and denial.

We feel frustrated and powerless.

We try to make things happen rather than be open to receive what comes.

We lose a balanced perspective.

We become more subjective than objective (lose our ability to detach).

We grab at apparent solutions and limit ourselves rather than giving ourselves options.

We become passive, passive/aggressive, and/or aggressive.

We set up situations that reinforce our low-trust viewpoints and expectations.

We get stuck rather than move forward.

We allow ourselves to be victimized and we victimize others.

We live a lot in fantasy and lessen our touch with reality.

We get into black-and-white thinking and behavior.

We become dependent rather than independent.

We become deceptive rather than straightforward.

We run from problems rather than face them.

We make mountains out of molehills.

We get into grandiosity.

We lose our emotional energy.

We lose our love.

We run before we walk.

We keep silent when we need to speak; we speak when we need to keep silent.

We complicate rather than simplify our lives.

We blame others for our dilemmas.

We become filled with emotion and lose touch with our rational selves.

We become willful and resistant to change and growth.

TRUST - in ourselves, in others, and in God is crucial to recovery.

Nonexistent Trust

Some people develop feelings of paranoia when their trust has been thoroughly and consistently abused. These people "read into things" words that are never said, "overhear" things that are never spoken, and "see" things that never happen. There are now Adult Children jokes. If an Adult Child is in a room full of people and he sees two people talking in the corner, he thinks they are talking about him!

Another joke tells about the man who said, "It's a wonder I'm not paranoid, what with everybody after me."

Many years ago, a coworker, Clara, accused me of talking about her to Evelyn when Evelyn and I were standing six feet away from Clara in her kitchen! If I wanted to gossip about someone, I wouldn't do it while she stood six feet away. And the more amazing part about what Clara "heard" was that she said my criticism of her was in answer to a question Evelyn asked. The point is that neither of us was focusing on or talking about Clara, yet she perceived small talk to be an attack on her.

While I was completing this manuscript, I cleared my calendar of all appointments: doctor, chiropractor, beautician, and all of my private clients, giving them the reason. One male client said, "I'm angry with you because you keep canceling appointments on me [This was the first.]. I think you haven't canceled anybody else but me."

Many years ago, a young female coworker reported several instances in which other coworkers had attacked her verbally. Once I was present when the so-called attack took place, and she misquoted that speaker to me later. Then I wondered how many of those other episodes had taken place.

Feelings of paranoia can cause extreme distortion in the way we perceive people, experiences, and God. We can even think God is against us when we have a series of disappointing happenings.

In a "Golden Girls" episode on TV, Dorothy starts feeling fearful that Ma may not live much longer and takes her to Disney World for a weekend. Ma wants to go on the rides, but Dorothy keeps Ma "imprisoned" in the motel room the entire time to look at photo albums and reminisce about the past. Finally, on Sunday afternoon, just before time to leave, Dorothy agrees to take Ma on a ride. Just then a thunderstorm breaks. Ma points upward and says, "How come you always take her side?"

We need to fight paranoia because it can cripple our lives. Just as the alcoholic receives the recommendation to attend ninety AA meetings in the first ninety days of sobriety, some Adult Children need to attend a daily meeting of some type so they will have a regular "infusion" of balanced thinking to offset the distortion of paranoia.

According to Rosellini and Worden, people who have a low level of trust are likely to respond in one of these ways.

1. *Isolate emotionally.*—We cut ourselves off from others almost completely. On the surface, we have polite, nodding acquaintances with neighbors, coworkers, or store clerks. Others might even consider us to be charming and friendly. The reality is that we are alone and cut off from human relationships.

2. *Have superficial intimacy.*—We may engage in romances and friendships that appear to be close, but underneath the apparent warmth we keep constant guard. We protect ourselves with a brittle armor, kidding ourselves that we are not emotionally vulnerable. "Our romances may be based mainly on sex or money because those are the only ways we know how to relate to another person," say Rosellini and Worden.

Many Adult Children fear that if they express their inner feelings openly to another person, he or she will reject, ridicule, and/or abandon them. They believe they must always be in control of their emotions—and the other person's too—or something terrible might happen. They test the other, manipulate, blame, and give guilt trips. The result? The relationships are filled with conflict and pain.

An Adult Child can be married or have an intimate relationships with another but can possibly have feelings of loneliness and alienation because of problems with trust. A daughter, for example, can learn from a co-dependent mother that men, and husbands especially, cannot be trusted. Mother demonstrated that the way to get one's needs met from men was to manipulate and control. The daughter feels the obligation to fix all the problems in her marriage and refuses to talk openly to her husband about her feelings because of her feeling of rejection. She fears that if she shows her "bad" side he will leave her.

Lonely people can have many contacts with others but may still feel very lonely because they cannot enjoy and feel satisfied in their relationships.

Unwise Trust

Trust has its tricky side: Blind trust can bring harm. Blind trust without reason can leave one feeling scared and empty. Adult Children, on the one hand, can fear giving trust; on the other hand, they can be naive with regard to trust. They can trust too quickly which leads to self-destruction. Neurotic trust involves trusting indiscriminately, naively. The one who trusts, because he hungers for affection, overinvests in the trustworthiness of the other. This person feels devastated when the other person lets him or her down. In short, when people feel needy, they can allow untrustworthy people to take advantage of them.

Adult Children view life as all-or-nothing. Rokelle Lerner says, "People who perceive the world in black-or-white terms often trust their friends to an unrealistic degree, thus setting themselves up for disappointments that inevitably follow." She recalls a classic example of a thirty-two-year-old woman client who finally had made a good friend. The woman traveled a great deal in her business, so she called on this friend and asked her to take her to the airport. The friend was busy that day and couldn't do it. The client felt rejected. So, she ended the friendship.

Candy, twenty-five, a grandchild of an alcoholic, has had a history of operating out of blind trust. "Whenever I met a guy, I ignored my warning signals and asked no questions. In the face of evidence of his lying, I never asked, 'Is he telling the truth?' I projected my ideal onto him and believed what I wanted to believe.

"Occasionally, I would stop by one boyfriend's apartment during the day. If he took a shower, he would unplug the phone and take it into the bathroom with him. When I would ask why, he would say, 'Well, you know my parents don't like you. They might call and if you answered, they would know you are here.' I swallowed that.

"When I came in one day and found him and an old girlfriend asleep in his bed, he said she came by the night before for a 'friendly visit' and drank so much she passed out and had been asleep all night. I bought that lie too.

"My biggest mistake was when I got involved with a cocaine addict and dealer. I didn't know about his drug use in the beginning, but too many things made my alarm bells go off. I brushed them all aside. He needed money, so I gave him money. He promised that he could pay me back soon from a deal he was working on, but I never got back one cent of the seven hundred dollars I gave him.

"The last involvement I had with a man, I got pregnant. When I told him about it, he wanted me to get an abortion but I refused. He wanted to continue the relationship but would not help me in any way with the baby. I told him to forget it.

"My child is now two years old, and I have been without a man in my life for nearly three years. That's the best thing that has happened to me. I know now that I can survive without a man in my life. I don't believe I will trust so unwisely in the future."

Candy has had the same trust issues in her work history. "I got my present job through a 'temp' agency. My boss, Jerry, was charming until the job became permanent. When the 'honeymoon' was over, he started talking abusively to me. I believed his promises about the big bonuses I would make without checking out facts. The reality is that this is a dead-end job and I'm getting double-talk when I ask about the bonuses."

Woititz says Adult Children hold this myth: We will trust each other totally, automatically, and all at once. Trust, she says, builds slowly.

Children of alcoholic parents do not know how to trust appropriately and have feelings of paranoia and resist trusting others; yet intimate relationships cannot develop without trust. Woititz says: "Why not trust everyone and then discount those who violate your trust? It will take much less energy.

"If someone turns out not to be worthy of your trust, you will be disappointed but not be devastated. Disappointment is something you have learned to handle very well," she says.

Vigilant Trust

Rosellini and Worden suggest that we should develop *vigilant trust,* which strikes a balance between credulity and suspicion. "Vigilant trust," they say, "is founded on *realistic* expectations. We can stop expecting ourselves to meet all the needs and demands of a partner. We can drop the notion that a partner must constantly prove his or her love." We can apply the same principles in friendship.

Trust, these writers conclude, needs to be *intelligent, discriminant, and prudent.* "To accept people as they really are rather than how we would like them to be are the elements of vigilant trust," they say.

They advise that people define trust in *specific* terms rather than in *abstract* ideals. To do this, one might list concrete expectations, such as, "I want to trust you not to be overly critical, not to laugh at my mistakes, or find ways of making me feel small."

Sometimes people communicate their thoughts and desires with dramatic silences and vague gestures. From the facial expressions and body language of others, we also draw conclusions that can be way off the mark. The frown may be real, but it may have nothing to do with us. The other person has an entire inner world that is separate from those around him or her.

We need to communicate our thoughts and desires precisely with words. We need to ask the important people in our lives what they are feeling rather than play guessing games.

Balance in Trust

Rosellini and Worden say that balancing personal needs against the needs and desires of others holds the key to having healthy and satisfying connections with other people. The intimate balance occurs when a person cares for himself and others and learns to express his feelings openly and free from hostility. When that person listens to the other person, he is free from guilt, defensiveness, or trapped feelings.

Woititz says we need to narrow our requests for trust rather than making it all-inclusive. For example, in a relationship, trust means:

Your partner will not abuse your feelings, and you will show your feelings.

You will not abuse your partner's feelings, and he or she will be able to show them to you.

The other person will say what he means and mean what he says, and you will do likewise.

Your partner will not willfully hurt you and you will not willfully hurt him or her. It is important to say, "It hurt me when you said that," and for the other to say, "It's important for me to know that; I will try hard not to let it happen again."

Trust means the freedom to be yourself without being judged.

Trust means stability.

Trust means commitment to the relationship to the degree that the couple has agreed to be committed.

Trust means that confidences will be kept.

It is important for couples to discuss the difficulties they have with trust and acknowledge that it is something for which to aim. They need to commit themselves to working on trust on a step-by-step basis as the relationship develops. They need to recognize that trust is not something that can automatically be given to another person.

Regaining Trust

What can you do when you have gotten burned in an intimate relationship or a friendship?

Elizabeth, twenty-five, grandchild of an alcoholic, has had a series of relationships with males in which she was deceived. She received counseling from a female for a couple of years. She has requested a male counselor to work with her on issues of trust with males. A counselor functions out of a nurturing style, in part, and a male counselor could thus embody nurturing, stability, and trustworthiness for a client. This sounds like a solid plan for someone in Elizabeth's situation. Sometimes a male needs a female counselor for the same reason. One could join a coed therapy group and or a coed twelve-step group to gain experience interacting with persons of the opposite sex in a setting where members commit themselves to mutual caring.

Cheryl's father committed suicide when she was fifteen. That is the ultimate act of abandonment. Cheryl, now thirty-one, sees a male pastoral counselor weekly. "That man is there for me; he is on time;

he shows caring for me," she says. She is beginning to rebuild trust in males.

Trusting Ourselves

Adult Children have "harpies" sitting on their shoulders to accuse them at every turn. "I came from a large family," Marian reports, "a large, critical family. Even if several of the critics were off duty at any given moment, at least one was on duty. Whatever I said or did was criticized by someone. Whatever I do or think or feel now, the first response I give myself is a critical one. It is so hard to trust my inner guidance."

Adult Children can expend enormous amounts of emotional energy trying to make decisions: they vacillate, decide, change their minds, bounce back and forth. How can they learn to trust themselves more?

Here is a personal experience that illustrates the point. I serve as secretary on the board of an organization. The president and I were the only officers who came regularly, and at one Sunday afternoon meeting, she and I were the only officers who came. A board member and two prospective board members completed the group.

It seemed to me, based on my feelings, that the president discounted and rebuked me every time I spoke, even when giving a positive report. I said things to myself, such as, "Surely you are mistaken. You are being overly sensitive."

At the close of the meeting, I waited until everyone else left and told the president I needed to check out something with her and told her my perceptions. She confirmed them, saying that she felt tense about the absence of the others. I thanked her for hearing me out and for being honest with me. It was then, and then only, that I *believed* my own perception of reality! If she had denied what I "saw," I probably would have given myself discounting messages and *should* messages. I was willing to allow another person to tell me what I was feeling!

The following addendum to that episode illustrates taking care of oneself and setting limits. By the way my stomach felt at the end of my drive home, I recognized that I had not told the president how I felt about her behavior. I had felt such relief that she had validated my feelings that nothing else occurred to me at the time. I called her and told her that in the future I would not allow myself to be used as anyone's whipping boy and that if I saw that behavior happening again I would do what was necessary to take care of myself: I would quietly leave and resign as secretary.

Jerri cannot trust her inner dialogue. She cannot decide whether to stay at her present job where she is treated unfairly. The promised review and raise has not come through, and she must work on weekends because additional help has not been hired. One message tells her to find a better situation but an inner accusing voice says, "You're doing your usual job-hopping and running away from problems." Another voice says, "This job is not the best for you; you need to give yourself permission to change." How can she know which voice to trust?

If you find yourself in a similar situation, these actions may help you make a decision.

Check it out. Maybe the thought to change jobs is an impulsive one and would be self-destructive. Talk to others. Share your *feelings* with others in a recovery program. That can help you clarify what your basic needs are.

Get facts. Talk to others who know your career field. If Jerri learns that her treatment is standard for that field or if few openings exist in her geographical area, she can decide whether the hassles are worth keeping the job or she can give thought to changing careers. She could then develop a strategy for making that type of change: What training would she need? What time period would she be dealing with? If she learns that openings with better working conditions exist, she can make a change or request improvements from her present supervisor and make a final decision based upon the response she gets.

Distrust Impulsivity. Impulsive moves may not be best for yourself or for others. In place of acting on impulse, substitute developing strategies and writing specific steps to get from the starting point to the goal.

Maybe you act decisively in career matters but cannot trust yourself in personal matters. Again, talk with others. Ask them to share their own experiences with you. Adult Children live in social isolation, and one of the important steps in recovery is to break out of that isolation and start talking and listening to others. You get support and feed-back vital to identifying your feelings and getting courage to act on them.

Take Risks. People become paralyzed when they feel torn between alternatives and do not trust themselves to move. List all input and make a decision. The fear of "What if I do the wrong thing?" keeps many frozen. We need to make the move that appears to be best at the time; if it turns out to be unwise, we need to apply mercy to ourselves, forgive ourselves, and give ourselves permission to make a *new* decision. Adult Children can keep themselves locked into a hurt-ful position because they made an unwise decision. Decisions can be remade. Statements such as, "You've made your bed, now lie in it," make us think we cannot re-decide.

Give yourself positive strokes for small accomplishments. Being in a support group helps with this since others usually see your accom-plishments more than you do.

Use Positive Self-Talk. Construct affirmation statements with re-gard to trust.

"I am a worthwhile human being."
"My feelings are to be valued."
"I get input before making important decisions."
"I move forward confidently in life."
"I am a decisive person."
"I am merciful to myself."

Promise to love yourself even if you make a mistake.

Learn more about the condition of your parent. If he or she were an alcoholic, attend AA meetings to learn about alcoholism and meet other alcoholics. If he or she were mentally ill, learn about mental illness. Our distrust of our parents can diminish when we learn more about their personal tortures.

Fred, forty-four, found it intensely difficult to deal with his mental-ly ill mother. One day they had a clash at her home. As he drove away, feeling as if he were going to go crazy, he "saw" in his mind a movie-house marquis flashing these words: NOW YOU UNDER-STAND HOW YOUR MOTHER FEELS ALL THE TIME.

"That gave me a remarkable turning point in my attitude," he reports. "I was able to write my mother and tell her that although we don't always see eye-to-eye, I still love her."

It was a turning point in my life when I recognized, on a feeling level, that my father had his own torment—the overwhelming desire to drink—and that he did not intend to behave harshly toward me. He dealt with an inner hell that I now understand, and that helps me forgive him.

Trust in God

When we find it hard to trust people whom we have seen, how can we trust God whom we have not seen? Trust in God is foundational for recovery, yet that is hard to achieve.

A man fell off a cliff and grabbed a tree branch. Swinging, about to fall, he called out, "Help! Is there anybody up there?"

A voice from heaven answered, "This is the Lord. Do you have faith?"

"Yes, Lord, I have faith."

"Then turn loose of the branch."

After a moment, the man called, "Is there anybody else up there?"

Trusting God calls on us to "turn loose of the branch." And that is scary! The basic concept of faith and trust means that we go forth into the *unknown*. If we know what is ahead, then we are not truly exercising faith. We are then acting on what we know.

To what extent can we live with uncertainty and the unknown? How can we trust God when, according to our perceptions, humans have let us down?

Some people learn to trust when they have reached the end of their own resources. Exhaustion can lead one to say, "I am willing to turn my life over to God. I'm running on empty." Adult Children are controllers, and it is hard for them to turn loose as long as they have an ounce of strength. Emotional, mental, physical, spiritual fatigue can cause one to turn oneself over to God.

Hearing the experiences of others can aid in opening our minds to the conept that God may be trustworthy. In twelve-step programs, members speak about God and we can begin to think, "Maybe that kind of help is available to me."

Observing the events in their own lives can cause people to say, "You know, certain things have happened lately that must have come from God. There is no other explanation."

As Jesus said, faith is like yeast. Once we have only a tiny bit in our lives, it grows and enables us to trust God even more.

Interacting with other people who prove themselves trustworthy can help us learn how trust feels and can lead us to transpose that ability to trust onto a Divine Being.

Some people use a GOD BAG or GOD BOX. They place slips of paper in it containing concerns, agreeing with themselves to turn that matter over to God for thirty days. When they turn the problem loose, they see God working.

Learning to Trust

Fear of trusting can keep us from forming secure relationships. Learning to trust begins with trusting ourselves. By learning to trust, we open ourselves to opportunities for developing healthy relationships. We take another step along the path to recovery.

Activities

Write in this book or use a separate notebook.

1. Rosellini and Worden point out that people with a low level of trust tend to isolate themselves emotionally or to have superficial intimacy. To what extent do you identify with these ways of behavior?

_____

_____ .

2. Which of the behaviors under the list, "When We Cannot Trust" apply most to you?

_____

_____

_____

_____

3. To what extent have you, or do you, practice unwise trust?

_____

_____

4. What have you learned from past experiences in trusting unwisely?

_____

_____

_____

5. If you are married or in an intimate relationship, take a look at Woititz's list of how trust functions specifically. Would you like to discuss these items with your partner and agree to work on one or more of them?

6. How would you describe your present need in the area of trust?

_____

_____

7. What action plan can you set to work on that area?

_____

8. Plan to confront someone who discounts your feelings, attempts to control you, and/or gives you "should" messages. Your statement could go something like this: "I just need to tell you how I feel: when you do (or say) thus-and-so, I feel uncomfortable and unsafe, and withdraw from you. I don't need anything from you other than to be heard."

Accept the fact that this action may end the relationship.

9. Construct a list of affirmation statements that have meaning for you.

_____

_____

_____

10. To increase your trust in yourself, list seven major accomplishments in your life. Include emotional experiences as well as specific events. Example: I dealt successfully with breaking off an engagement with someone who really was not right for me.

_____

_____

_____

_____

_____

_____

11. If your trust level of God is low, write a statement to God, clarifying your position and your reasons for distrust.

_____

_____

_____

12. Write this Bible verse twenty-one times a day for twenty-one days:

"I will trust, and not be afraid" (Isa. 12:2, KJV).

Here are some other Bible verses to meditate upon:

"Lord, I believe; help thou mine unbelief" (Mark 9:24 KJV).

"Under his wings shalt thou trust" (Ps. 91:4 KJV).

"They that trust in the Lord shall be as Mount Zion which cannot be removed, but abideth forever" (Ps. 125:1 KJV).

"Whoso putteth his trust in the Lord shall be safe" (Prov. 29:25 KJV).

13. Commit to trust. Write out, "I choose to trust when faced with anxiety." Then ask yourself, "What actions can I take now that would be consistent with trust?"

7

Intimacy Issues

Adults from troubled families have severe difficulties in achieving *intimacy*—a feeling of being connected—with other human beings, whether on a friendship or a romantic level. Brenda Schaeffer, author of *Is It Love or Is It Addiction?* says that intimacy is a profound expression of our identities, in which the persons exchange thoughts, feelings, and actions in an atmosphere of openness and trust that leaves them in a euphoric state. This exchange involves the Natural Child in the two persons. A *true* marriage contains intimacy. Many marriages are legal unions but would not qualify as real marriages. The partners rarely touch each others' *hearts.*

What is meant by *intimacy?*

In *The Art of Intimacy,* Thomas Malone and Patrick Malone say that our *intima,* which means the innermost part of ourselves, lies inside each of us. This is the seat of our deepest feelings, motivations, our values. It contains our behavior that expresses these qualities.

Knowing yourself is the basis of intimacy. In homes of trauma, an individual doesn't develop a firm *self,* nor does he spend much time inquiring into his *self.* He focuses almost entirely on another in order to keep himself safe.

There is a saying, "There must be a *me* before there can be a *we.*" Many times a person tries to link with another person in an intimate experience before he has developed a *me.* So one task to take care of before even attempting to link up with another would be to work to develop a *self.*

Being in touch with another is the outstanding quality of the intimate experience. It takes place along with our opening ourselves up when in contact with another person. It feels good, real. Eric Berne, author of *Games People Play,* says that we experience about three hours of sustained, true intimacy in our entire lives.

Personal Space and Intimacy

Everybody has a sense of personal space. When we are there, we feel comfortable about who we are without being defensive. We rarely spend enough time there due to the business of our daily lives and due to the fact that we bring too many people in to help us feel secure. How crowded is your personal space with people and ghosts of people past?

Healthy people go back and forth from personal space to shared space throughout the day. A person whom we would describe as mature can be himself at the same time that he is in a relationship with another. It is possible for someone to remain in his personal space while being with other people but it is difficult.

The main question is: When we are in a relationship with another person, how can we be ourselves? The most difficult task for couples is finding how they can move with ease and trust from being in the shared space to being in the personal space.

The only way intimacy can take place is when you remain *yourself* and move into the shared space with someone who remains *himself or herself.* Intimacy means that two people can be in each other's space without thinking they must change the other or themselves. Each can remain who he or she is and be valued for that.

A person whom we would describe as neurotic feels the need to accommodate, compromise, or change who he is in order to maintain a relationship, even though the relationship may be uncomfortable, unsatisfying, or even abusive.

A neurotic always lives in the shared space; he never has any personal space. He exhausts himself by staying almost totally in the shared space. He is unable to make a choice about when to move in and out of his personal space, thus he loses his ability for spontaneity. He is a prisoner of his need to be constantly observing and responding to the other person.

The main concern of a neurotic is, "What do other people think?"

He agrees within himself to live his life in terms of how other people respond to him. Thus it is impossible to be who he really is since how he acts and feels depends on others' expectations of him for him to know who he is. "If you want me to be vivacious, I'll be vivacious; if you want me to be subdued, I'll be subdued. Just tell me what and I'll deliver it."

Neurotics feel confused and sometimes betrayed when people don't respond positively to their placating and compromising. A young man considered himself to be a perfect date: prompt, attentive, sober, compliant. "Why won't a girl ever go out with me twice?" he wonders.

A neurotic gives away his personal space out of resentment and anger because he is dependent. He adjusts his own self to "take care of" the other. The healthy person gives away his personal space by choice.

Dependent, addictive, hysterical, or compulsive persons stay in the shared space too long. Usually the only time they are in their personal space is when they daydream and fantasize. A person who is addicted to a chemical withdraws into a distorted internal space; a depressed person withdraws into his own space.

"Simply put, the neurotic or psychotic condition is the partial or total inability of the person to be himself in the presence of others. *He can be a virtuoso at accommodating his feelings and behaviors to his sense of the other person's needs, but know little of who he really is,*" say Malone and Malone. A psychotic cannot be in relationship with another person in any way. He always lives in his personal space. A psychopath does not live in either space.

Caring of Versus Caring for Others

People get confused between love and "taking care of" a dependent person. Taking care *of* is not the same as caring *for* someone.

Caring *for* others is nearly always the opposite of taking care *of.* The latter diminishes both persons because it is patronizing rather than being mutual. It can be tolerating (which is a superior rather than equal position) rather than accepting, and pity is sometimes involved. Resentment and anger can be present also.

Malone and Malone write, " 'Taking care of' " is close, not intimate; it is like providing a service. It does not build or change relationships. Closeness affirms and sustains a relationship." *Intimacy changes relationships.*

Closeness Versus Intimacy

Closeness and *intimacy* are not the same thing. Being close jeopardizes one's personal space. Family members who have excessive closeness stop "seeing" each other. "We didn't know our older adolescents were using heavy drugs. How could we have missed that when we are so close?"

"Closeness is what you feel and experience with another in the shared space," say Malone and Malone. When close, you are slightly more aware of the other than of yourself. "If the other is *immensely* more important, yours is not a healthy closeness, and you have a problem." There needs to be a balance in how much each gives: The one who gives away too much of himself in closeness is out of balance; the one who can give nothing is equally out of balance. Unhealthy closeness causes each to be neurotic when with the other. Neither changes, therefore neither grows.

People learn about *themselves* when *intimate;* they know the *other* when they are *close.* Intimacy nourishes people in ways that closeness cannot.

We usually think of *closeness* as a positive characteristic in a relationship. A mother may say, "My daughter and I are very close." Yet the two may have constant conflict. Excessive closeness means that the two are heavily enmeshed; it probably is not healthy. Likewise, two people who never have conflict speak about how close they are. Probably the two merge as one personality rather than there being two separate selves choosing to relate. In short, we value "closeness" when upon examination, some very close relationships do not offer health to either person.

"The power of love depends on the *balanced* interaction between being close and being intimate in our relationships. Intimacy is *one* dimension of real love," Malone and Malone say.

Being "In Love" and Intimacy

What people call being "in love" is not the same as love and it is
not intimate. When someone is "in love" with another, he idealizes
the other and loves that ideal rather than the real person.

M. Scott Peck, in *The Road Less Traveled,* describes what happens
when two people "fall in love." People feel lonely within their personal boundaries and long to connect with other people. Falling in love
allows them temporarily to come outside. That experience causes a
person to drop a portion of his boundaries, invite the other into his
personal space, and to blend his identity with the loved. This brings
about a release from loneliness and from oneself.

Janet Woititz, in *A Struggle for Intimacy,* says that in the early
stages body chemistry is activated and each person is extremely attentive and involved, which produces intense feelings. She compares it
to the energy one feels in a crisis. Each wants to fuse with the other
which causes powerful emotions. She calls this stage an "involvement" rather than a "relationship." The closeness feels good, and
each feels flattered by the attention received from the other.

To an extent, the act of falling in love causes the person to regress,
to go back to infancy. A young child feels omnipotent, and falling in
love produces that feeling. Outsiders may be able to see horrendous
obstacles ahead for the couple, but they themselves feel all powerful
and believe that love can conquer all. This feeling is unrealistic and
compares to the grandiose feelings of a two-year-old who believes she
has all power.

After the initial stage of oneness that brings feelings of euphoria,
the realistic stage appears. A couple simply cannot sustain the intensity characteristic of a beginning romance. The pace must slow down.
Each can feel rejected, disappointed, depressed. The excessive involvement with the other becomes suffocating and draining. The couple
discover that they are more different than each had thought: Each
wants to do a different thing at the same time; each holds a different
value on a certain topic. Traits and foibles that seemed "cute" in the
beginning now irritate. Each starts feeling critical of the other. They
start viewing each other through the eyes of reality rather than fantasy

as before. Their boundaries snap back into place gradually or suddenly, and they start trying to change each other.

Bradshaw explains that during courtship, each person is free to view the other separate from the issues of each family of origin. When the wedding takes place and the two become husband and wife, all of the unresolved family issues come into play.

What do they do? Do they get into a power struggle where one wins and the other loses? Do they make personal attacks on each other?

Elwin treated Ann like a queen during their courtship and had a high level of trust toward her. He had not resolved his issues with his mother who controlled the family a great deal. After the marriage, Elwin's "tapes" started playing, "A wife tries to control her husband." Although Ann is a complex person who approaches Elwin and expresses herself in a variety of styles, he views her exclusively as, "You're trying to control!"

Ann feels confused. The man who put her on a pedestal has become an adversary against whom she feels the needs to defend herself.

The stage of being "in love" lasts from eighteen months to two years, so after that period of time, each falls "out of love." Some couples divorce at this point and those who have a greater degree of emotional maturity start to work at real loving.

Peck says, "It is when a couple falls out of love that they may begin to really love." It is his position that real love does not have its roots in a *feeling* of love. "Real love often occurs in a context in which the feeling of love is lacking, when we *act* lovingly despite the fact that we don't *feel* loving," he says. Why does Peck take the position that falling in love is not real love?

He points out that falling in love is not an act of the will, that it is not a conscious choice. A person can fall in love with an extremely unsuitable person while failing to fall in love with someone the person admires and wishes to fall in love with. Falling in love "happens"; real loving takes effort. Real love calls on a person to extend his boundaries; falling in love causes a collapse of one's boundaries. Real love calls for discipline; people who are lazy and undisciplined can fall in love. Real love extends one's boundaries and causes them to remain in that larger position which enriches the person. Falling in love does not enlarge a person; he does not grow through this experience.

Real love concerns itself with the development of the other; falling in love takes place to help ease the person's own loneliness. In fact, people who are "in love" feel so content and view the other as being so perfect that this experience does not motivate either to work on development of self or the other.

Peck concludes that "falling in love" relates primarily to a physical, sexual attraction that creates an aura of euphoria for the lover. "Couples who stay in therapy learn that a true acceptance of their own and each other's individuality and separateness is the only foundation upon which a mature marriage can be based and real love can grow," Peck observes.

Intimacy and Sexuality

Intimacy may be sexual, but sexuality is not the heart of intimacy.

Janet Woititz in *A Struggle for Intimacy* says that sexual intimacy is one means of communicating and sharing yourself with the other. The sexual behavior of the couple is a symptom of whatever else is happening with them.

Woititz calls on us to look at what we learned about sex in our homes. She points out that in an alcoholic home, in particular, the viewpoints about sexuality were distorted, which can create confusion about sexuality. "What did sex mean to your parents?" she asks.

A female client told me, "My mother didn't want to have sex with my daddy because he always lay in bed drunk." One woman saw that her parents fought and then made up in the bedroom. She learned, "You use sex to end an argument." Woititz says that sex can be used to avoid problem-solving rather than enhance the relationship. A woman taught her daughter to give men sex because it put them to sleep.

In some homes, sex is a power and control issue. It can be linked to physical abuse. Some feel powerful and in control in the bedroom. One woman said, "It makes me feel sad that the only thing I think I have to offer is my body." Another woman saw lovemaking as a violation in her home, and that blocked her wanting to share herself sexually with her husband.

Survivors of incest face formidable obstacles in feeling comfortable with healthy sexual behavior. Emotional incest takes place when a parent places a child in the sweetheart place in his or her life instead of the spouse. Trust in adult relationships becomes a major issue for incest victims.

Children who grow up seeing one parent cheat on the other invariably find this dynamic being played out in their lives. They get cheated on by their partners.

The bottom line is, "I am afraid to get close. I may get hurt and I may hurt you."

Difficulties in sexual attitudes and behaviors can be worked through. Trust, shame, control, boundary, self-esteem, rejection, abandonment, and anger issues all express themselves in sexual behavior.

One partner may ask the spouse to get help from a sex therapist because the couple has difficulty in that area. The complaining partner may say, "That's the only problem we have. If we can straighten that out, everything will be fine."

The spouse may respond, "We have problems in many areas. The only time he takes me seriously or turns his work loose is when he wants to have sex with me. I feel used and resentful that he is not there for me any other time."

Resolving sexual problems requires looking at the complexity of the couple's entire relationship and at the attitudes each partner brought into the marriage. Unresolved resentments toward parents can play themselves out in the bedroom of a couple of a later generation.

Acceptance in Intimacy

God models the true meaning of grace. He loves others completely, in spite of their behavior. There is no intimacy without grace in our personal relationships. When humans accept another unconditionally, they exhibit grace. Malone and Malone say, *"Acceptance is a fundamental precondition to intimacy."* Usually, each individual is saying to the other, "Be what I need you to be and then I can accept you."

Accepting another means accepting the other's *feelings.*

People are born with *primary feelings,* such as fear, anger, sexuality, elation, and curiosity. Families teach children *metafeelings.* Metafeelings are learned feelings, the feelings we have about our primary feelings. Metafeelings may be negative, such as shame, guilt, hostility, and hopelessness; or they may be positive, like modesty, gratitude, and consideration.

"Knowing" Others in Intimate Relationships

Malone and Malone say that our "knowing" of others blocks intimacy. They define "knowing" as *prejudging* another. Bonnie says about her husband: "I know what he is like. I know what he is going to say before he knows it." Individuals stop really hearing or seeing the other because they "know" in advance.

A husband accused his wife of being dishonest because she told him she went to her room for needed quiet after their exhausting day of buying two cars. "I *know* you!" he said in my presence in a counseling session. "You get hung up every time we spend some money and you were mad about that!" Even though she insisted that she didn't feel angry about the money, he *knew* what she was feeling and attacked her. "How can we move forward in our relationship if you won't be honest?"

Prejudging another sets up expectations, a self-fulfilling prophecy; the other then usually meets the prejudged expectations. Because of this "knowing" one another, couples get bored and seek out the unknown.

"Once you prejudge your spouse, your sexuality is limited. You can make love only within the confines of your judgment of how he or she, or you, can or will be." Malone and Malone comment. "Sex is a rerun, no longer fun, exciting, passionate."

Blaming and Intimacy

Blaming is deadly to intimacy. Blaming—a strong metafeeling—claims the right to say how the other can be and not be. In human relations, there is little that is *cause and effect,* which leaves little room for blame. People interact with each other and each participates in what happens. When a person is blamed, he inevitably becomes defensive. *When I stop blaming and recognize that I am the only one I can change, intimacy can take place.*

Individuation and Intimacy

One of the most important tasks a child has is to *individuate,* or *differentiate,* from his parents. That means for the child to become an individual he needs to develop an identity that is strictly his own and is not a copy of one or both of his parents. He develops boundaries that define him as an individual. This need comes into play heavily during adolescence and brings about much of the conflict between parents and adolescents. For the sake of the child, this healthy individuation must take place.

David D. Waanders says that individuation of self is essential to develop a healthy intimate relationship with another. In short, children cannot develop intimate relationships with other children, even though those "children" may be six feet tall and twenty-five years old.

Adults who have achieved individuation can relate freely to another person in mature patterns and are not bound by dependency needs and insecurities. For example, Jan has a pattern of moving from one intimate relationship to another, like stringing beads on a necklace. She is "in love" with men in rapid succession. Jan, daughter of an alcoholic father and a mentally ill, physically abusive mother, has high dependency needs. Is it possible that her "I love you" translates into "I'm very needy and I feel so scared when I'm alone that I will attach myself to any male"? As one of my professors in graduate school said about individuals who marry many times, "The names are changed to protect the guilty."

A female client said to me, "I married the same man three times." She amended, "The first time his name was Sam, the second time it was Bernie, the third time it was Lee."

The puzzle analogy is used to explain this pairing. As we come out of our families of origin, we have a "shape" that defines how we fit into our family puzzle. We float around looking for a person whose puzzle shape fits ours. We may have too little personal identity to make a mature choice about pairing with the other person.

The opposite of differentiation is *emotional fusion*. In the Bell curve, the hump rises in the middle and each equal side gradually curves to the ends of the line. To understand emotional fusion, draw a horizontal line and move the hump to the far left end of the line with a gradual decline toward the right end of the line.

The hump on the left side represents the majority of the population: people who have little *self*. People in the left half operate more by feelings than by reasoning. These individuals spend much of their energy seeking love and approval, and they attack others when they don't provide it. These persons, therefore, have little energy to move toward goals and to make choices.

"These people become victims of others and of circumstances," Waanders says. "They are vulnerable to anxiety and dysfunction if change occurs because they feel threatened. They either avoid relationships for fear of getting into uncomfortable fusion or they continue to pursue enmeshed relationships."

What happens when an individual from the left end links up with another intimately?

She will pair with a person of the opposite sex who has an equal status of differentiation (a status which is practically nonexistent). Waanders says, "Persons tend to marry partners who are on the same level of differentiation as themselves." These two individuals form a couple, and they fuse into one being. The lower the level of personal maturity, the more intensely these persons mesh. They have little sense of personal boundaries.

In ordinary arithmetic, one half plus one half equals a whole; but Waanders says that in these cases, each person is a half self. Multiplication operates rather than addition: one half times one half equals one quarter. The two become less because they do not bring two whole selves to the union.

These partners have few skills to interact, to set goals, or to solve problems and work as a team. One usually emerges as the dominant decision maker, and the other agrees to adapt; or a passive spouse forces the other to become dominant. A power struggle takes place when both partners try to dominate.

When tension arises, the emotional fusion heightens conflict. This couple might separate to put some distance between themselves, but they remain emotionally fused even when apart. Each remains in the other's mind obsessively.

A fused couple goes through cycles: They are very close at first; they have conflict; they put distance between themselves (literal or emotional); then they make up. The cycle begins all over again.

When conflict comes, each focuses on the other and thinks the way to end conflict is to get the other person to change. Each tries to blame the other for the deficiencies within himself or herself. Possessiveness, pain, and chaos characterize the relationship.

Waanders says, "When individuals grow in differentiation, this will strengthen them in their general functioning and can make the marriage better."

What about those few people on the right end of the line? In one of my seminars, someone asked, "Aren't those people lonely over there by themselves?" The people on the left end are lonely but keep themselves enmeshed with others so they delude themselves about their loneliness. The people toward the right end have more energy available to pursue goals, therefore, they derive more satisfaction from their actions, says Waanders. "These person are in charge of their own lives, and in intimate relationships, they are freer to give themselves to others."

Play and Intimacy

What is the *only thing* you can *do* to be intimate? *Play,* Malone and Malone say. "Do not prejudge; then you can behave spontaneously." They give four requirements for learning to play:

—give up the need to win;

—give up the need to be first and so enjoy just being;

—give up the need to be in control and so enjoy the other;

—just enjoy the game.

To play, we must be willing to follow whims.

Malone and Malone say that in relationships and marriages, people struggle more with others than play with them. They wind up in chronic low-level struggling that takes the place of play and kills intimacy.

Opposite Pulls in Intimacy

Janet Woititz, in *A Struggle for Intimacy,* says that we feel pulled in two directions when it comes to intimate relationships; we want the person to come closer but we also push him or her away. That push/pull feeling gets in the way of getting what we want in relationships. She says that we need to acknowledge the feelings, turn them loose, and put new viewpoints in their place.

Myths Regarding Intimacy

Woititz identifies myths that Adult Children of Alcoholics hold regarding intimacy in relationships.

MYTH: "If I am involved with *you,* I will lose *me.*"

TRUTH: Healthy relationships enhance the self and do not absorb it.

A person who reaches *maturity* along with achieving *adulthood* usually lives by his inner voices which are stronger than those outside. This allows him to hold onto his own identity while being intimately involved with another. This can happen only when the individual has developed a strong sense of self, which is difficult when growing up in an alcoholic home.

Emotional immaturity leaves a person vulnerable to giving oneself away, so the fear of losing oneself in a relationship has realistic roots in the past. One has to examine, however, the reality of the present situation. Maybe it is not like the past. Therapy or involvement in a support group can help you check out reality.

MYTH: "If you really knew me, you wouldn't like me."

TRUTH: Your beloved probably already really knows you and cares about you anyway!

We walk around as though the CIA, the FBI, and the KBG were following us! At any moment, we fear that we will be found out. We need to learn to take risks, to be who we are and accept the consequences. A relationship based on falsehood is not worth having, anyway. If the other wants you only when you present a perfect facade, do you want that other person?

MYTH: "If you find out that I am not perfect, you will abandon me."

TRUTH: Perfection does not exist.

Since abandonment is our greatest fear, we project that onto intimate relationships. Projection leads us to bargain with the other, in which we agree to be perfect rather than real.

The fear of abandonment can cause us to throw aside the real issues that need to be dealt with.

MYTH: "We are as one."

TRUTH: You are you and I am me, and then there is us.

We rush into bonding with the other. Genuine, lasting relationships take time. Trust develops slowly rather than happening instantly.

MYTH: "Being vulnerable always has negative results."

TRUTH: Being vulnerable sometimes has negative results and sometimes has positive results, but it is the only route to intimacy.

We feel out of control when we make ourselves vulnerable. We can then feel powerless to prevent bad things happening to us. The only way to develop healthy intimate relationships is to share our feelings with our partner. If that seems to be too risky, an intimate relationship is out of the question. Woititz says, "The idea of being vulnerable may be more terrifying than the actual experience."

MYTH: "We will never argue or criticize each other."

TRUTH: Couples argue from time to time and are critical of each other's behavior.

Adult Children fantasize and come to believe that an ideal relationship contains no conflict. Their fear of anger and angry people makes them shrink from incorporating all dimensions of emotions into their personal interaction. They push down their anger and deny it. Sometimes this leads to depression.

Adult Children often think, *If the other gets angry at me, she/he doesn't love me anymore.* If they feel angry at the other, they think their own love has died. It is hard for them to conceive that love and anger can be present at the same time.

Elwin grew up watching his parents bicker over trivial incidents and quarrel over major issues all of his life. He thought, *If I love my wife, I will never get angry at her; and if she loves me, she will never get angry at me.*

After Elwin and Ann returned from their honeymoon, he said, "I want us to never get mad at each other." Anytime Ann delivered a legitimate complaint about Elwin's behavior, he accused, "You're angry at your husband!" and made that the focal point, rather than dealing with her frustration. He acted as if being mad at one's mate was some sort of crime.

Elwin, of course, could not keep his side of the agreement, but it threatened him too much to acknowledge his anger. He handled it by withdrawing from Ann and by being sarcastic.

As Adult Children, we lack skills in problem-solving, so we avoid anger. It does not seem possible that anger can be resolved without real or symbolic bloodshed. Woititz says, *"Anger is an ever-present, hidden issue in the relationships of Adult Children."*

MYTH: "Anything that goes wrong is my fault. I am a terrible person."

TRUTH: Some things that go wrong are your fault. Some are not. Terrible things happen, but you are not terrible.

Adult Children personalize conflict and place blame rather than looking objectively at what is happening and searching for resolutions.

MYTH: "In order to be lovable, I must be happy all the time."

TRUTH: Sometimes people are happy, and sometimes they are not.

Adult Children carry a lot of sadness from the losses in their families, yet they felt pressure at home to always be "up." They fear that showing sadness will drive the other person away.

MYTH: "We will do everything together—we will be as one."

TRUTH: Couples spend time together, alone, and with friends.

MYTH: "You will instinctively anticipate my every need, desire, and wish."

TRUTH: If needs, desires, and wishes are not clearly communicated, it is unlikely they will be fulfilled.

In every relationship, each person has expectations. In a committed relationship, each pledges to try to meet expectations. The question is: Do we tell the other what we want or expect the partner to read our minds? Partners will disappoint, but when people care about others, they work hard to make those events minimal.

MYTH: "If we really love each other, we will stay together forever."

TRUTH: People stay together and people separate for many reasons.

Adult Children sometimes stay in marriages that are destructive. A wife may allow herself to be beaten and continue to stay in a marriage out of loyalty. When the daughters of that couple grow up to be battered wives and the sons grow up to be battering men, the cycle is perpetuated.

MYTH: "If I am not in complete control at all times, there will be anarchy."

TRUTH: One is in charge of one's life and takes control of situations, as needed, by conscious decision and agreement.

There are also times to share control and times to give up control. Couples involved in a healthy relationship do not get into power struggles. The two can give and take and neither has to do it all.

MYTH: "My partner will never take me for granted and will always be supportive and noncritical."

TRUTH: Things do not always go smoothly, but you always have a right to your feelings.

Feelings need to be expressed. After that, the person often doesn't feel a need for the behavior to change.

Millie spent all of her free time with her alcoholic mother who was dying of cancer. Her husband felt left out and angry and complained. Millie defended herself and attacked him. If she could have validated his feelings, maybe he could have supported her behavior. If Millie could have said, "I understand how you feel. I'm sure I would probably feel the same way. This is difficult for me too; I feel torn between two people I love. It's just that, in this case, I feel I must give first attention to my mother. I hope you can understand and support me."

Validation does not mean agreement. It means respect for legitimate differences. It is the cornerstone of good, solid communication. Without validation, communication is merely a power play, Woititz says.

Developing Intimacy

As we come to know ourselves, we develop an increasing capacity for intimacy. Intimate experiences enable us to touch and be touched by others. Learning to be intimate with friends and family moves us closer to healing.

Activities

Write in this book or use a separate notebook.

1. To what extent do you think you have developed a "me"?

2. To what extent do you feel comfortable staying in your personal space?

To what extent do anxiety feelings push you to always be in the physical presence of another?

3. Define the difference between "taking care of" someone and *caring for* someone.

4. What persons in your life do you "take care of"?

5. What persons in your life do you *care for?*

6. Are you and anyone else in your life too close as defined in the chapter? (You do not really "see" the other, "hear" the other, etc.)

7. To what extent to you prejudge (by "knowing") a person with whom you are intimate?

8. To what extent do you try to change the other person rather than take responsibility for changing yourself?

9. Plan a schedule for play for the next month.

10. List the myths you feel apply to yourself.

_____

_____

_____

_____

8
Parenting Issues

When I teach seminars on parenting, I prefer to present concepts which provide a framework for parents to develop their own skills. Because personalities come in such an endless variety of forms, it is difficult to say, "Do this, do that, and all will go well with your children."

When I face a group of parents, however, they sit with hopeful, uplifted faces, pens and notebooks in hand waiting for me to give them THE ANSWER about how to get effective results with their children. And it is fair to expect an instructor to give some specific parenting guidelines.

So, from my point of view, parenting needs to be approached from two angles: parental issues and parental skills. The issues lay a groundwork for developing skills.

Task of Parenting

Ted, newly married, took his bride for their first visit with his parents. As the couple talked about their plans for children, Ted asked, "Dad, what's it like being a father?"

Ted's query caught the older man off guard. "It's like lighting a candle," Dad began. "You shelter the flame for a while, and then you must step away and let it glow fully, no matter the circumstances. Knowing when to step away . . . is the tough part.

"It's a feeling I can only describe to you, Son. It is not something I can sing, write, or say to you. You will understand when your day arrives."

M. Scott Peck in *The Road Less Traveled* says: "The job of a parent is to be of use to a child. It is to encourage a child along the path toward independence." He describes parents as "executives, and despite the fact that they are usually ill-prepared for it, their task can be every bit as complex as directing a company or corporation." (Amen! *My comment.*)

If some parents put the same amount of thought, planning, and effort to parenting as they do to their careers, they would have greater success as parents. People expect good parenting to "just happen." Many parents do not *abuse* their children, but they practice *lazy parenting,* which brings ineffective and/or destructive results. Parents who take the easy way out often pay a price later by going to court because of difficulties a child gets into, paying bills when a child goes into drug treatment, and enduring personal pain due to the conflict within the family.

Walter Delamarter, executive director emeritus of the Florida Baptist Children's Home said, "A parent's main task is to *enjoy* his children." Often well-meaning, conscientious parents work so hard at the job of parenting that the children do not get any feeling that the parents enjoy *them* as persons.

I open a seminar by telling parents that if they do the following three things they will do an effective job as parents:

1. Resolve all unresolved issues with your parents.
2. Resolve all unresolved issues with yourself.
3. Resolve all unresolved issues with your spouse.

At this point, the students in the seminar feel emotionally overwhelmed and just sit with glazed looks in their eyes.

Unresolved Issues in Parenting

All unresolved issues with parents, self, and spouse play themselves out in parenting. When a parent asks for help regarding a child's behavior, he or she typically reports an incident as isolated and asks, "How do I handle that type of behavior?" or "Why does my child act that way?" A behavior that emerges in a single incident often has complex roots and expresses many issues.

Walter, thirty-two, comes home from work bringing the news that he did not receive the promotion he had dreamed about and expected.

He feels frustrated, disappointed, hurt, and scared. He had counted on the increased income to lessen financial stress. How will he and his wife handle their financial obligations?

This incident dealt a blow to his self-esteem. How will this affect his career future? He had told his perfectionistic dad (who lives nearby) about the promotion, and Dad will probably criticize him for failing to make the grade.

When he comes in, needing to talk to his wife, Celia, she cannot give him immediate attention. She got home from work late and is rushing to cook supper. On one level, he acknowledges the reality of the situation and pitches in to help get the meal; on another level, he feels hurt and angry that she doesn't drop everything to attend to him.

Before the family can eat, Walter's parents drop in unannounced to hear the good news, so supper is delayed. Celia feels annoyed because her retired in-laws know that she and Walter work and that they need to take care of dinner at this time, yet these drop-ins at an inconvenient hour take place on a regular basis. She has complained to Walter and expected him to set some limits on his parents; he has been unable to, so Celia feels angry at both her husband and her in-laws.

During the visit, Walter's middle child, Kenny, starts teasing his little sister, something he does habitually. That gets on everyone's nerves. Walter and Celia have found no way to curb that behavior.

Walter "blows up" at Kenny, whacks him soundly on his bottom, and yells at him to go to his room and stay there until he can "behave right."

Celia defends Kenny and argues with Walter: "Well, he is tired and hungry! What do you expect?" She hopes her in-laws will take a hint and leave, but they stay.

Walter's father says: "The kid deserved what he got. That's exactly the way I handled you when you were little, Walter. And it didn't hurt you a bit."

How did both Walter's and Celia's unresolved issues with themselves, their parents, and each other affect their son's behavior and the way they handled it?

Resolving Issues with Parents

Lets take a look at how resolving issues with one's parents can affect one's own parenting behavior.

In *The Dance of Anger,* Harriet Lerner tells about a woman named Maggie whose parents had divorced. Mother expected Maggie to side with her and to alienate Dad. Mother, bored and depressed, spent a great deal of time at Maggie's home and interfered with her raising of her daughter, Amy.

Maggie worked with Dr. Lerner until she could speak calmly to Mother about how important it was to Maggie to do what she thought was best with Amy. She asked Mother if she would stop telling her what to do with her child. Mother responded with hostility, and Maggie was able to remain firm yet courteous.

Maggie continued to work on changing the old pattern. Sometimes she slipped back into fighting, instructing, and criticizing her mother. She got herself back on course each time, however. This led to a new adult relationship with Mother. Maggie started to ask her mother more about her early life and her relationship with *her* parents. Mother's previous offensive and irritating behavior became more understandable. Maggie saw that Mother truly desired to help and that she was also afraid of losing Maggie.

Maggie attempted to reestablish contact with her father. He resisted and moved further away emotionally. She continued to write to him and to stay out of the fighting between her parents. Eventually the relationship with her father strengthened.

Dr. Lerner says: "If Maggie had not done this work, she would in time have found herself overinvolved and intensely reactive to one or more of her children. Or, alternatively, she might have been overly distant and emotionally cut off when her children were grown, which is simply the other side of the same coin. *Although Maggie is not yet aware of it, the work that she did is the best 'parenting-effectiveness training' that money can buy."*

Maggie's story shows how resolving issues with one's parents relates to disciplining one's child.

Resolving Issues with Oneself

When we have low self-esteem or confusion about our own identities, we act those issues out with our children. We may become perfectionistic, expecting them to compensate for what we see as our own inadequacies. We can be overly critical of their shortcomings because they remind us of our own. We can take out our frustrations on our children because they are handy. We can extend little mercy toward them when they make mistakes if we judge ourselves harshly for errors.

The story about Walter and Celia illustrates the need to resolve issues with oneself in order to be a better parent. If Walter blamed himself for failing to get the promotion, he might react in a negative way toward a failure of a child.

The more we can accept ourselves as we are, warts and all, the more we can value our children as they are, warts and all. We will expend our emotional energies and efforts toward building relationships with our children and supporting them in their struggles rather than causing division, hostility, and chaos within the family.

Resolving Issues with Spouses

Children become frequent and convenient dumping grounds when a husband and wife have unresolved issues between them. Parents suppress anger toward a spouse and direct it toward a child. Parents attach themselves too closely to children when they feel frustrated and needy in their marital relationships. Parents call on children in open and subtle ways to take sides with one against the other.

Patricia came to me for counseling. After holding in her anger toward her husband for years, she had decided to get a divorce. She described the family: a teenage girl, an eleven year-old boy, and a younger girl. "My husband treats the girls well, but hates our son," Patricia reported. "So I try to make it up to him." She did not realize that her compensating behavior hurt her son more than it helped him. An unhealthy bonding existed between these two as they aligned themselves against the "wicked enemy."

Commitment to Growth

M. Scott Peck talks about the importance of parents being willing to change so they can respond adequately to children's needs. Children change constantly, and a stagnant parent lacks insights and skills to deal effectively with children at their current level. Barbara functioned at a high level with her children when they were small. When they entered adolescence, she tried to continue treating them as she had when they needed more parental care and supervision. She and the children were in perpetual conflict. The children chafed at her hovering style of mothering, and she chafed because of their resistance. Just when parents think they "have a handle" on the stage their child is in, he shifts to another stage! How frustrating!

Adult Children Issues in Parenting

Control, intimacy, and trust are the three main issues for Adult Children. All of these display themselves prominently in the parenting arena.

We believe we should be in control. How do we feel when we feel out of control with our children? Helpless. We globalize: We think of all that is going wrong with the children rather than focus on the isolated incident; we think it is our fault; and we get angry at the children for making us feel helpless and looking bad in our own eyes and in front of others.

When a child with a problem approaches us or if we learn the child is doing something wrong, the parent's internal "tapes" usually start playing something like this:

"I've got to solve this, and *now!* "

"This will reflect badly on me."

"It's all my fault."

"My child is bad" (therefore, I am bad).

We then go into action:

We blame and lecture.

We get on the phone.

We write letters.

We visit teachers and counselors.

We may even hit the child.

We rearrange our lives to solve the crisis.

We think we must have instant answers when something goes wrong at home. We bark out an impulsive order, criticism, or blaming attack. We say things we regret and do damage to the child, ourselves, and the parent-child relationship.

It's OK not to be in control as a parent. It's OK to tell the child you need time to think about how to deal with her when she has done something intolerable. Maybe a teenage daughter comes home late and drunk. The best thing to say is: "Go to bed now. We will talk to you later." When a crisis arises, it is appropriate—and fair—for the parent to take time to think and develop a strategy.

Can you begin to feel comfortable saying to your children, "I don't know what to do in this situation"? *Invite the children to participate in problem-solving in the family.* They can contribute creative and workable solutions.

Intimacy with Children

We long to have intimacy with our children; we can feel pulled toward them and can push them away at the same time. We can give them mixed messages. Toni finds herself snapping at her child just when they start sharing and giving each other affection. "I start feeling claustrophobic," she explains, baffled at her own reactions. "He looks hurt and confused at my sudden change."

Trust Issues with Children

Our problems with trust can lead us to have a high level of paranoia toward our children. "I always think my son is trying to put one over on me," Toni says about her four-year-old. "I wind up accusing him of doing things that I'm sure he never thought of doing. When I blow up at him, he gets quiet and stays out of my way. Then I feel terrible."

Setting Limits with Children

One of the greatest needs in effective childrearing is for parents to set firm limits. I identify this as my greatest weakness as a parent. I could say the words: "Hear ye! hear ye! If you do thus-and-so, thus-

and-so will result," but then I overidentified with and felt sorry for the child in pain and withdrew the consequence.

How can a parent set limits when he has a weak sense of personal boundaries? When a parent lacks boundaries, he can become enmeshed with the child and attempt to meet his needs through the child. He cannot see clearly that the child needs limits and cannot value the principle that limits ultimately make for a happy child.

I learned the value of limits for children in a surprising way. Someone gave our daughters a poodle when they were teenagers. Because the girls were gone all day, the dog became attached to me. He responded beautifully to limits and seemed to be happier and calmer when I operated within limits. He got frustrated when I operated outside of limits. Because I could view the dog with more objectivity than I could my children, I saw the value of limits in a way I had never seen before.

When Adult Children who are parents start making progress in their recovery, setting limits for their children becomes easier.

Representing God to Children

A child's religion develops not so much by what parents say but by what they do, says M. Scott Peck. This exchange took place between Peck and a grown male client:

CLIENT: "I have this notion of a cutthroat God but where did it come from? My parents believed in God—they talked about Him incessantly. Jesus loves us. God loves us. We love God and Jesus. Love, love, love, that's all I ever heard."

PECK: "Did you have a happy childhood?"

CLIENT: "Stop playing dumb. You know I didn't. You know I was miserable."

PECK: "Why?"

CLIENT: "You know that, too. I got the _____ beaten out of me. Belts, boards, brooms, brushes, anything they could lay their hands on. There wasn't anything I could do that didn't merit a beating. A beating a day makes a good little Christian out of you."

The client came to believe in what Peck calls the "monster-god."

A child's first idea of God's nature comes from a blending of his two parents' natures. A child who has loving, forgiving parents is likely to develop a view of God as loving and forgiving. The child will likely view the world as a nourishing place the way his childhood is.

Parental Misbehavior

Much of a child's misbehavior comes from adult misbehavior. The child does something that would not happen if the parent set up the scene with thoughtfulness and consideration of the child. When the child annoys the parent, the child gets punished.

Darlene, a divorced mother who is lonely and in need of adult companionship, picks up her two small girls from the day-care center at the end of her day's work. She is exhausted and has a "short fuse." She stops by a friend's house for a brief visit to meet her own needs. The children—tired, hungry, and in need of Mother's attention—get fussier and fussier. Darlene continues to tell them to leave her alone. She eventually spanks each child for "misbehavior."

In this case, the adult has legitimate needs but the children get branded as "bad" and get hurt. If Darlene could have arranged to take care of the children's basic needs first and then take care of her own, things probably would have gone more smoothly.

When my daughters were very young, I was amazed when they said one day, "Grown-ups are better than children." We act so righteous when disciplining children and place so much blame on them that they—with their limited cognitive skills and undeveloped emotional selves—believe what we say to them: "This is your fault. I don't want to spank you (send you to your room, make you go to bed early, etc.) but you made me."

Treat Children with Respect

We need to commit ourselves to treat children as people. Where do we get the idea that we can or should treat children as other-than-people? We speak to them, use eye expressions, hit them, and do things to them that we would never do to a friend, a fellow worker, an employee, our own parents, a sibling, or a stranger who asks for directions. What makes us think that just because a human being is young and small he will respond positively to intimidation, bullying, ultimatums, ordering, insults, shouts, rage, and hits?

Parents need to make a primary task of helping the child develop trust in them. Predictability, which comes through consistent behavior, builds trust. When a child has developed trust—one of her primary developmental tasks by age five—she will usually cooperate. A balky child typically has a trust problem.

Parents Teach By Being

Dedicated parents take their job as teachers seriously. We tend to think, however, that we teach a child by what we *say*. We teach much more by what we *do*. What do your children learn by what you do? If one day's activities could be filmed and you could view your behavior through the child's eyes, what is she learning from your facial expressions? body language? voice tone? actions? responses to other people? confrontations with others? or lack of confrontations? Does your child see you always apologizing and taking the blame, justifying, giving defensive responses to others?

How does your behavior affect your child's self-esteem?

How does your behavior affect the parent-child relationship?

Does she see you behaving in a hostile manner and delivering anger inappropriately? (A five year-old girl asked her mom, "How come you're always fighting with everybody else?")

How often does she see that your facial expressions, tone of voice, or body language contradict your words?

Taking Care of Yourself

Adult Children parents make great Martyr Parents. That makes us feel so good but that behavior brings disastrous results. Repeat after me: "I will be a better parent if I am good to myself."

Activities

Write in this book or use a separate notebook.

1. Make a list of the unresolved issues you have with your parents.

_____

_____

_____

_____

2. Make a list of the unresolved issues you have with yourself. Example: "I still haven't forgiven myself for having premarital sex."

(A family came into counseling because the parents learned their seventeen-year-old daughter was having sexual relations. The mother behaved so hostilely toward the girl in sessions that the counselor saw the parents separately. The mother revealed that she "had to get married" to her husband because she was pregnant at seventeen. She had never forgiven herself and was taking out her own unresolved issues toward herself on the daughter).

_____

_____

_____

_____ .

3. Make a list of the unresolved issues you have with your spouse.

_____

_____

_____

_____ .

4. Write a statement of your values and expectations for yourself as a parent.

_____

_____

_____

_____ .

- your feelings as a parent.

_____

_____

_____

_____ .

- your behavior as a parent.

_____

_____

_____

_____ .

- your goals for yourself as a parent.

_____

_____

_____ .

- your goals for your child (children).

_____

_____

_____ .

Evaluate your statements: How realistic are they? What perfectionistic expectations toward yourself does it contain? What pressure would that put on your children?

_____

_____

_____

_____ .

5. List some things you can do to treat yourself better.

_____

_____

_____

_____ .

6. Evaluate the time you spend with your children:

What percentage of time do you spend "working your children over" about behavior and how much time do you spend relating to them?

_____

How much time do you give at meals to focus on behavior? (correct young children's table manners, scold them for not eating, etc. My personal opinion about teaching manners compares to teaching a child correct grammar. If the parents speak correctly, the children will speak it; if the parents use correct table manners, the children will, too—eventually. It may not happen as quickly as you would like, but poor table manners in a preschool child is not a terminal disease.)

_____

Do you use mealtime to hold "family court" and drag children before the judge or do you keep that time exclusively for enjoying the family?

_____

7. Make a list of things you would like to do for personal enjoyment. If it is hard for you to do that type of thing, list the items in order of strength, from easy-to-do to very-difficult-to-do. Make a contract with yourself to do at least one of the easier activities within the next week. You may need to stay on an easy level for a few weeks until you feel comfortable, then move up a level at a time.

_____
_____
_____
_____ .

9
Parenting Skills

"Love and good intentions aren't enough to discipline children," says Nancy Samalin in *Loving Your Child Is Not Enough.* "We also need skills."

Paul offers sound instructions for families. "Children, obey your parents; this is the right thing to do because God has placed them in authority over you. Honor your father and mother" (Eph. 6:1-2, TLB). He goes on to say, "And now a word to you parents. Don't keep on scolding and nagging your children, making them angry and resentful. Rather bring them up with the loving discipline the Lord himself approves, with suggestions and godly advice" (v. 4, TLB).

Learning About Children

A mechanic who intends to do an effective job must know about engines. A parent who wants to do an effective job needs to know about children. We parents often approach our task with little knowledge about the "engines" we will work with. Here are some of the things we know about children:

• Children come into the world equipped to recognize their own needs and to get their needs met for food, sleep, relieving discomfort and pain, for getting nurture.

• They know how to express feelings freely and accurately. Adults rarely have to guess how a baby feels: whether it be sad, confused, afraid, tired, or angry. Babies show feelings by facial expressions, voice, tones, or body language.

• When a child trusts, he usually cooperates.

- Children respond well to order and structure (limit-setting and boundaries).
- They respond well to positive, precise directions.
- They respond well to eye contact and touch.
- They respond well to encouragement.
- Their actions generally make sense when you understand their point of reference. (This does not mean you must give in to a tantrum, for example, but understanding may help you feel less annoyed at your child's behavior.)
- A child is a walking recording machine, observing, learning, and repeating. He seems to walk around taking notes and thinking, *Oh! This is the way it's done. And that is the way I must do it.* Many times conflict occurs between parents and a child when she repeats what she observed. The parents say, "Where in the world did you learn that?" and punish her.
- Children do not respond well to scolding. (Does anyone at any age?)

Effective Parenting

Samalin says the effective parent nurtures, helps, supports, gives affection, expresses feelings openly, encourages children to express feelings openly, leads in resolving conflicts rather than avoiding them, and communicates honestly and constructively. People handle feelings in three ways: talk them, repress them, and/or act them out.

When families are not open and encouraging, members do not discuss feelings or resolve problems and children behave in negative way to get attention (act out feelings).

The effective parent is fair and flexible. He holds expectations that are clear and free from hidden motives. The expectations take into account the child's age, skills, and where he is in his developmental stage. The ineffective parent expects too much, too little, or is inconsistent.

The effective parent includes all the children when making rules and decisions. Ineffective parents do not allow little children to participate in decision making. In one family, Dad asks, "Where do you all want to eat?" as they make plans to go out. His wife suggests

Chinese food. "Aw, there's no good Chinese place in town," Dad counters. The seven-year-old son votes for Mexican food. "Who wants to eat a lot of beans?" Dad sneers. "We want to eat something more elegant than that when we go out." The twelve-year-old daughter wants to eat pizza. "We are going to a restaurant, not a fast-food place," Dad tells her. In the end, the family always goes to the place of Dad's choice.

The effective parent gives positive input to the child. This input:

• makes the child feel that he is a unique individual who has his own identity,

• makes the child feel valued in the eyes of his family,

• makes the child feel his parents trust him to make decisions on his own and to solve problems, and

• builds the child's self-confidence.

The effective parent gives positive nonverbal messages to a child by smiling, touching, and making eye contact.

The effective parent eliminates verbal punishment which includes nagging, lecturing, name-calling, sarcasm, and intimidating tone of voice.

The opposite parental behavior ignores the child and emphasizes his negative behaviors and personality traits.

Types of Parenting Styles

Here is a description of three types of child-training.

Authoritarian

The authoritarian parent places the child in an inferior position. The child may become discouraged, fearful, and people-pleasing.

Kevin Leman, in *Making Children Mind Without Losing Yours,* says that the authoritarian parent sees himself as better than the child. The parent rules the home with an iron hand, grants little freedom, and makes all decisions for the child.

The authoritarian parent relies heavily on Ephesians 6:1-3, which says children are to obey parents. He rarely acknowledges Ephesians 6:4 that admonishes parents not to provoke their children.

Pampering, Overprotective

The pampering, overprotective parent places the child in a superior/inferior position. On the one hand, the child rules the home and the parent is a slave. This parent, says Dr. Leman, places priority on the child, not on the spouse, and robs the child of self-respect and self-esteem by doing things for her that the child can do for herself. On the other hand, the parent retains control: He rarely grants the child any freedom away from the parent. He makes things as easy as possible—does for the child, answers for the child, and so forth; yet denies freedom. This inconsistent parenting style invites rebellion from the child.

This parent anticipates the child's needs and provides them so the child does not have to initiate requests, and the child becomes passive. The child feels he can't do anything unless the parent is handing out praise.

When a parent overprotects, he interferes with the child's developing self-esteem and a feeling of competence.

Democratic or Responsible

Democratic parents operate by this guideline: "Parents have *more experience* and take the *leadership* role." They take the responsibility of showing their children where the fences are. They offer choices and formulate guidelines, says Dr. Leman. They hold the child accountable and let reality be the teacher.

Children take responsibility for their actions, including taking the consequences for mistakes. Parents do not intervene between the child's behavior and the reaping of the results. This calls for the parent to "sit on his own pain" while letting the child reap his own pain.

This type of parent uses the consequences of reality to teach the child. *Consequences come in two flavors: natural and logical.* A natural consequence takes place when a child does not do his homework and reaps the results at school. A logical consequence takes place when the parent sets an agreement ahead of time relating to cause and effect. The agreement needs to be as specific as possible. If the child "forgets" to take care of his hamster, the parents will give the pet away. One mother told her nine-year-old son she had given away his hamster because of his neglect. When the boy defended himself, Mother said, "The hamster has been gone two weeks."

The crucial element in using consequences as the primary disciplinary tool lies in the parent's ability to stand firm when the time comes to apply the results. If the parent weakens, the child learns that the parent threatens but does not carry through.

I was an prime example in the weakening department. (That could be an entire book by itself!) When I felt strongly enough about something to carry out the agreement, I would say, "This time I mean it!" to differentiate from the other times. The children learned when to carry out responsibilities and when they could get by without complying.

The responsible parent values the child's feelings and treats him with respect. The responsible parent lessens her share of decision making based on the child's age and maturity.

Maintain Objectivity

Adult Children can experience paranoia in all relationships, including those between parent and child. We can take things personally when the behavior of the other person reflects what is going on within that person rather than how he or she feels toward us. When a parent puts distance between himself and his child and relates to the child on an objective basis, the parent-child relationship improves. This can be difficult to do.

When I talked about this concept in a seminar, a woman said testily, "When my six-year-old son says something mean to me, there's no way my feelings aren't going to be hurt." In this case, the objectivity principle calls on the parent to ask herself, What could be going on in my child that would make him yell, "I hate you!" The next step is for the mother to talk to her son about why he feels upset. The more parents think along these lines, the less they will feel hurt.

Dealing in information helps a parent stay objective. Samalin tells about a nine-year-old boy who asked his mother if she would cook cheese and eggs for his breakfast. Mother complied and set the plate before the boy who then said, "I don't want that."

"Oh," Mother replied calmly, "I thought you did." (She thought he did because he said he did, but she continued to deal with information.) "I cook breakfast only once," she said and calmly left the room.

It was her son's turn to say, "Oh." He then had three choices: eat the eggs, prepare something different, or go hungry. He ate the eggs.

Importance of Communication

An effective parent communicates expectations clearly rather than over using *no*. A child is more likely to follow instructions that use:

• a precise vocabulary (rather than a general, "Behave yourself!") and step-by-step directions rather than "Toilet-train the puppy,"

• a respectful tone of voice, and

• a positive statement of what you want rather than a negative one of what you don't want. For example, "Leave that alone," rather than, "Don't touch."

The following guidelines will facilitate good communication:

Avoid the use of the verb *to be* when speaking to and about a child.

Avoid: "You are messy."

Say: "You must clean your room."

Avoid: "You are hogging the phone."

Say: "I want you to wind up your phone conversation within five minutes; I need to use the phone."

Avoid: "You are stubborn."

Say: "You have two choices about what to do; which of these do you choose?"

Use of the verb *to be* focuses the child rather than the behavior. The use of that verb also locks the child into a rigid pattern and limits the way the parent sees him. Sometimes a mother is overheard saying, "Toby is my difficult child." Such a statement locks the parent into viewing that child in only one dimension; it sets up an expectation and the child lives up to that expectation.

Communicate clearly, briefly, positively rather than negatively, and in a firm, friendly tone of voice.

Avoid ultimatums ("Do that or else . . .") and threats ("If you don't, I will. . . ."). Don't paint yourself into a corner or set up a situation that invites the child to defy. Threats and logical consequences differ primarily in the way they are set up. Consequences take place in an atmosphere of negotiation when parents are calm. Threats take place when the parent is agitated and often says things he regrets and does not carry out.

Give specific directions. Tell the child what to *do* rather than scold. Focusing on the negative behavior encourages its repetition. "I want you to do. . . .' works better than, "Will you stop . . .!"

State your position clearly and avoid vague communication which forces the child to read between the lines. The child can misinterpret and do what he thinks is pleasing the parent and can miss the mark because of a faulty assumption.

Sometimes parents scold and punish children when the parent never gave instructions. Saying, "But I thought you would know not to do that!" assumes the parent knows what the child is thinking.

When our oldest daughter was ten, we visited my sister whose son had recently broken his leg. Our daughter found his crutches fascinating and walked around with them. The family lives in an old farmhouse with a long flight of stairs. When my daughter took the crutches upstairs, it occurred to me to warn her not to use them on the stairs, but I checked myself with, "She is such a sensible child, she won't go on the stairs." Within a few minutes we heard a terrible clatter and rushed to the hallway where she lay on the floor, extremely scared but unhurt. Rather than comfort her, I scolded her. I erred in assuming that a responsible child, in general, knew how to handle a specific situation.

Effective communication makes statements. In many instances, a question is a backhanded complaint and addresses a vague issue that is difficult for the child to answer. "Why did you come home late?" is asked when a parent's really means, "I'm angry because you broke curfew." "Why are you still watching TV?" is asked by a parent who wants the child to turn off the TV and do something else. "Why haven't you done . . . .?" reflects a parent's need to give directions for the task, to invoke the consequences that follow, or tell the child the parent needs time to think of logical consequences.

Other questions that do not communicate include "Can't you be nice to each other?" "Shouldn't you wait until after lunch to eat that

candy bar?" "What's the matter with you, anyway?" "Didn't you
know to do . . .?" Do not ask, Why? Deal with behavior.

Commit to Making "I" Statements

When people get into conflict, they usually analyze and blame
others rather than making an *I* statement about their position. One
of my daughters confronted a young man who rents a room in the
house where she lives. He was habitually leaving the front door un-
locked and running the air conditioner on cool days or when the
windows were open. She approached him in a calm, direct, nonaccus-
ing manner and asked him to please take care of those items.

He responded, "You're the kind of person who bottles things up
and you need to tell other people things right away!"

All of you, dear readers, have witnessed (and participated in) identical exchanges. The analyses and blaming swing back and forth.

I have made a commitment to make *I* statements. Recently, I
confronted another daughter about something that bothered me. She
responded with an "analyze and blame" statement. My commitment
made me pause long enough to think before speaking rather than
responding emotionally and making a personal attack. *I* statements
focus on the issue rather than dissect the other person.

The parent does not have the power to control a child's behavior;
the child may test the limits even when the parent practices positive
communication skills. By using clear communication, however, the
parent is behaving in a healthy manner and the results are more likely
to be positive. Children echo what they hear from their parents;
positive communication will develop eventually; the parents may hear
it when their children talk to *their* children.

Whose Problem Is It?

Parents can't always fix problems for their children. There is only
100 percent space for worry about any problem. The more the parent
agrees to worry about the child's problem, the less the child does (or
can since that "worry space" does not exist.) The parent needs to ask:
Whose problem is this? the parent's? or the child's?

Effective parents pull back in their agreement to worry about their children's problems. They ask, What can you do about this problem?

A parent who overfunctions produces a child who underfunctions. The parent eventually gets angry that he is overloaded; it is within his power to change the pattern of behavior.

Parents of an elementary school boy received a letter threatening to put him off the school bus due to disruptive behavior. "Allen," Dad said after showing his son the letter, "you have a problem. We live too far from school for you to walk, and I am not going to drive you. What do you plan to do?"

Allen thought a moment, then proposed, "I could sit at the front behind the driver away from the other boys. That way, I wouldn't get into trouble."

"Fine," Dad agreed.

The next morning, Dad walked with Allen to the bus stop and explained the plan to the driver. The plan worked, and Allen had no further problem.

Let us review the steps Dad took.

1. He clarified who had the problem and observed boundaries.

2. He dealt in *information* rather than *emotion.*

3. He used positive communication skills: He did no name-calling and did not humiliate his son.

4. He took his own position and set limits: He would not allow Allen to walk, and he would not protect his son by driving him to school.

5. He took a supportive position to Allen as he worked on his own problem.

6. He did not allow the incident to ruin his day.

Another parent might not handle the situation so well.

How would an average parent handle such a situation?

1. He might take the problem on himself and get upset.

2. He might blame the child and punish him. Perhaps he would also scold him, attack his self-esteem, make a self-righteous speech about how good the parent was as a child, or ground him.

3. He might hold onto the anger toward the child for a period of

time and allow his feelings about that incident to spill over into other areas.

4. He might solve the problem himself, often to his own discomfort, such as disrupting his schedule to drive the child to school.

5. He might protect the child, by driving him, which would remove the child from the setting and rob him of an opportunity to develop skills in problem solving.

In the school-bus situation, the relationship between Allen and his dad did not suffer any damage; rather, it deepened. No verbal abuse took place; Dad did not get angry at Allen. Dad communicated respect for and trust in Allen by depending on him to come up with a resolution. Dad praised Allen for working out a solution. Surely Allen had good feelings toward Dad for the way he handled things. When a parent gives a child the opportunity to make decisions for himself, the child develops inner responsibility.

The emotional and physical health of the family increased through this exchange. No one's body produced chemicals that contribute to ailments caused by emotional stress. Dad didn't work on an ulcer that day!

Focus on Task

When a parent gets angry at a child because a task was not done or was done poorly, the parent often focuses on the child with belittling words, threats, physical hitting, and other punishments. In the end, the task often goes undone and the parent-child relationship is fractured.

If the parent can train herself to focus on the task and picture herself calling on the child to join her shoulder to shoulder to accomplish that task, tasks will get done more efficiently and relations will improve within the family. Call on the child to put his shoulder to yours and focus on the task by asking, "What is the best way to get this done?"

A friend of ours did a good job in this respect with his three daughters. He would say, "OK, this is what needs to be done. What is the best way to do it?" He would supervise as the sisters negotiated and developed a strategy.

Focus on New Behaviors

People can start new behaviors more easily than they can eliminate undesirable ones. Tell the child what you want and reinforce those behaviors with praise.

Listen

Listening to children teaches them their value in a powerful way. Some parents do not have the ability or do not want to give the energy needed for true listening.

M. Scott Peck says:

> The more you listen to your child, the more you will realize that your child has valuable things to say. And the more you listen, the more you will know about your children and will be able to teach them more appropriately, and the child will not turn a deaf ear. The more the child knows you value him, the more willing he will be to listen to you and value you.
>
> The need for one's parents to listen is never outgrown.

A thirty-year-old talented professional man went to Dr. Peck for treatment of feelings of anxiety related to low self-esteem. The young man could recall numerous instances in which his parents, also professionals, had been unwilling to listen to what he had to say. At twenty-two the client wrote a thesis that earned his graduation from college with high honors. His ambitious parents were delighted by the honors their son had received. He left a copy of the thesis in full view in the family living room and made frequent hints that they "might like to have a look at it." Yet neither read it. He refused to beg them and was hurt deeply.

Parents name their reasons for not listening to their children: It is boring, inconvenient, and takes energy.

Peck says that because his parents loved and valued him as a young child, he felt secure enough to question their expectations and depart from the pattern they had laid out for him when he was older. He felt worthless and crazy in doing what he did, but on a deeper level, he sensed himself to be a good person. . . . He responded to earlier loving messages from his parents which said, "You are a beloved individual. We will love you no matter what you do, as long as you are you."

Peck says: "One of the most valuable, and cheapest, services we can perform for our children is to listen. Period."

Listening—without comment—gives the child an important sounding board to hear himself. Listening out loud to oneself helps to clarify one's issues.

Listening—without comment—gives the parent time to clarify the issue and to still his own swirling emotions so he can think and act more clearly.

Listening—without comment—shows the child you value him.

Listening—without comment—increases the bond between the parent and the child.

Listening—without comment—communicates to the child that you trust him to work on his own problem.

Listening—without comment—models rational, respectful behavior before the child. He will give that behavior back to you one day. Hysterical behavior on the part of parents usually comes home to roost.

Burton Hillis wrote in his monthly column in *Better Homes and Gardens* that his fourteen-year-old son talked to him about his dilemma—which girl to ask to a party. The son wanted to invite a girl who was not popular, and his friends were pressuring him to invite another girl. Hillis listened only. The boy, by thinking out loud, concluded that he wanted to invite the girl of his choice. "Thanks, Dad!" he called, as he walked away. "You were a big help."

Choose Your Fights

Parents need to select which incidents are worth fighting about and which have no long-lasting consequences. A rigid parent can fight with a child about everything. One mother picked at her son until he finally did what she wanted. Then she attacked him about his motive. The son could never win!

Winnie regarded her eight-year-old son as difficult in shopping for his clothes. They argued about what he should get: the parent's ideas of what looked good versus the child's idea. Cost was not a factor—

what each wanted cost about the same. The son simply wanted to be in style with his peers.

Mother said, "There's nothing neater than navy blue shorts."

James answered, "That's your opinion. I want jams."

Mother argued, "If you ask Daddy, I'm sure he will agree with me."

"That's Daddy's opinion," James replied.

Much emotional energy and time are wasted arguing fine points that really are not relevant. Adult Children parents get into controlling and try to convince the child to do what the parent wants when the issue at stake is irrelevant.

Guidelines for Parental Action

Here are some guidelines in taking action in a child's behavior: Is the behavior hurting the child? Anyone else? Property? Does it violate some strong value of yours? Often the child's behavior is not wrong; it is annoying or inconvenient to us at that moment.

Take Care of Your Own Needs

Balance—important in any endeavor—is especially important in parenting. Martyr parents can become abusive parents. Dr. Leman said that when his first child was born the doctor gave the parents an important piece of advice: "Start going out one night a week as soon as the baby is a few weeks old." The doctor placed high emphasis on the marital relationship. Parents who have a strong marriage will come nearer doing an effective job of parenting than those who do not.

Another important parenting task is to take good care of individual needs. If a parent lives through a child, both the parent and child will be hurt.

What About Hitting Children?

I intentionally did not use the word *spanking*. We react differently to the word *hitting* versus *spanking*. Many parents who advocate spanking recoil with horror at the thought of hitting a child and would condemn parents who hit. What is the difference?

A spank is a hit, however we may clothe it. I advocate no hitting (except when a child is in danger). Here are some reasons I take this position:

We become hysterical if anyone outside the family hits one of our children. In a North Carolina town where my family lived, a woman teacher with years of quality service in the school system grabbed the upper arm of an eight-year-old girl just before the children left the room one afternoon. The girl went home crying and showed bruise marks to her mother. The issue inflamed the community, and parents insisted that the teacher be fired. The school board met until 4:00 a.m. deciding the question, and the pastor of my church cast the only dissenting vote against firing.

We demand that other caretakers of our children discover and use disciplinary methods that do not include hitting. Why should family members be the ones who have the privilege of hitting other family members? An international report on family violence commented, "For some, there is more safety on the streets than in their own homes."

The idea of hitting a child grows out of a centuries-old idea that the wife and children are a man's property and that he can do with them as he wishes. Just as he might hit his mule, he could likewise hit family members.

Slapping in the face humiliates in addition to hurting physically. Hitting a child in front of others is also humiliating.

We teach children not to hit others, especially those who are smaller; and if we hit them, we are teaching that it is OK for the strong to hit the weak. Perhaps we have all observed a child hit a younger child followed by a parent hitting the hitter, saying, "Don't hit some-one smaller than you!"

A young brother and sister squabbled. The boy pulled his sister's hair, and she bit her brother. Daddy said, "I'll teach you how that feels." He bit the daughter and pulled his son's hair. "And," he reported proudly, "they have never done that again!"

Children do, indeed, "learn," from such parental intervention, but they do not learn skills in solving problems and handling frustration and anger. Nor do they learn what it means to be grown-up if parents act on the same level as the children. Adults need to behave on a higher level than children.

A survey showed that, in the United States, people touch primarily to hit each other or to engage in sexual activity and/or abuse. Sometimes the only time a parent touches a child is to spank him.

When a parent hits a young child he learns, "The people who love you sometimes hurt you." Children who are hit grow up to be parents who hit.

Dr. Leman says:

> The Scripture tells us to be in authority over our children, but it doesn't say to be *authoritarian.* The authoritarian parent often backs up his "I know best" attitude with force, but that's not what the "loving discipline" of Ephesians 6:4 is talking about. Perhaps the most misused (not to mention misquoted) verse in the Bible is, "Spare the rod and spoil the child." The actual text reads: "He who spares the rod hates his son, but he who loves him is careful to discipline him" (Prov 13:24, NIV).
>
> The Jews believed in discipline, but when biblical writers used the word *rod* they were thinking more of correction and guidance than hitting and beating. For example, the shepherd used his rod not to beat his sheep but to guide them. We are all well acquainted with that phrase from the Twenty-third Psalm, "thy rod and thy staff they comfort me" (v. 4). But I doubt that many of us would feel very comforted if the Lord's rod was waling away at our heads or bottoms at every wrong turn we made.

Carolyn DeArteaga, Christian counselor in Marietta, Georgia, says, "The 'rod' represents authority. A parent who hits his child to make the child do what he wants creates a child who learns that one hits to get what one wants. I counsel parents to use spanking as an absolute last resort."

Parents who commit themselves to the no-spank rule develop a wider repertoire of approaches to use with their children than parents who believe in spanking.

When a parent hits a child when it is a matter of safety or by accident, the child usually does not feel "hurt" physically nor does he resent it. Spanking hurts the child's feelings as well as hurting physically.

The behavior modification theory advocates hitting a child—*once*
—to save the child who is in danger or when it is necessary to get his
attention to tell him something important. A counselor friend of mine
thumps his son on the top of his head to get that kind of attention.

If we hit a child, what does he learn about us, others, and God?
Discipline is primarily a matter of demonstrating love to our children.
C. Sybil Waldrop wrote in "Where Discipline Begins," *Home Life*,
August 1987:

> We usually think of *punishment* when we use the word *discipline*.
> Discipline teaches. Punishment is used to stop behavior.
> Disciplined parents will want to apply these guiding truths:
> It is the job of the parent to take care of the child. The strong are
> to take care of the weak.
> Children do not come perfected. Parents are co-creators with God
> as they guide the development of the child. A perfectionistic view
> toward children implies that they are fully formed.
> A child is a gift of God.
> A child is made in the image of God.
> A child is not an adult.
> A child is not an extension of the parents but is a separate individual.
> Parents are to be an example.
> The Golden Rule is a guide for relating to our children. We discipline
> more by example and relationships than through words or actions.

Dealing with Younger Children

With young children, we need to deal objectively with behaviors.
The parents need to set limits on behavior but not on feelings or
expression of feelings. The story that follows illustrate these guidelines.

Claudia, a four-year-old, became a dictator with her divorced
mother, Alicia. Whenever Alicia had a date with her new boy friend,
Carlos, Claudia began to "sob mournfully" and treat Carlos rudely
by refusing to speak to him. Claudia sometimes had a temper tantrum.

Alicia tried to reason with her daughter by telling her that there was
no reason for Claudia to be upset about Mother going out with Carlos,
that soon Claudia will get used to Mother going out and it will no

longer bother her. Mother explained that Carlos is a nice man and that with effort, Claudia would come to like him.

Claudia wouldn't listen. She climbed under the covers or put her hands over her ears or cried louder. One time she behaved so badly that Mother canceled her plans.

Alicia felt sympathetic with Claudia's unhappiness over the divorce but felt furious at what she called the "dictator."

According to Dr. Lerner, reasoning with children is trying to convince them to see things our way. Alicia wanted to date Carlos and wanted Claudia to be happy about that. Lerner points out that whenever a child expresses sadness, anger, hurt, or jealousy, many parents move in to do something to make the child feel better. "Emotional overfunctioning reflects the fusion in family relationships. Family roles and rules are structured in a way that fosters overly distant fathering and overly intense mothering."

Lerner says that when parents "stay in their own skin" children can handle their own feelings, discover solutions to their problems, and develop skills to ask for help when they what it.

Alicia first changed her response to Claudia's behavior. She listened to her daughter's feelings and made statements that did not try to change Claudia's feelings. She acknowledged that Claudia felt angry about Mother going out and that the little girl did not like Carlos.

Second, Alicia took responsibility to decide whether to date Carlos no matter how her daughter felt about it. She said, "I know you are feeling upset because I'm going out with Carlos, but I am going out and I will be home at 11:30. You will be asleep then and I'll see you in the morning."

Third, Alicia made rules about how Claudia could act and set consequences if Claudia broke the rules. Claudia would be taken to her room and would have to stay there until she calmed down if she threw a tantrum. Alicia told Claudia that she did not have to talk to Carlos if she did not want to but that she must tell Carlos directly rather than just refusing to speak.

Alicia and Carlos had tried to force Claudia to like Carlos, the child had backed off. As the adults softened their agenda, Claudia behaved in a friendly manner to the man.

Dealing with Teenagers

As children mature, parents need to relate to their teenagers on a more mature level. Several areas illustrate the potential for a changing relationship.

Express Feelings

With older children, the parent can express his own feelings of hurt and disappointment more than with younger children. "I'm feeling hurt by what you are saying."

Use Parallel Communication

In *Stop Struggling with Your Teen,* Evonne Weinhaus and Karen Friedman advocate using *parallel communication.* For example, Mother comes in from the supermarket and says, "The groceries need to be brought in." Teen: "But I'm on the phone."

Ordinarily, Mother starts arguing with the teen. "But the groceries need to be brought in." When we use the word *but,* that implies that our need is of higher value than the teen's. This sets our agenda as more important than the teen's which causes him to reach negatively. (Our agenda may be more *urgent;* for example, the frozen food may need to be put away right away.)

Parallel communication would go this way: Mother, "You are on the phone *and* the groceries need to be brought in. They need to come in within ten minutes because of the frozen food." Parallel communication places the two agendas on the same plane, and the teen does not feel the need to get defensive.

Use Appropriate Discipline

Weinhaus and Friedman name the following methods of discipline that parents use with teens:

Grounding,

Guidance—trying to persuade the teen that what you want him to do will pay off for him in the long run,

Supervision—the parent takes responsibility of seeing that the teen does the task,

Understanding—the parent asks the teen to talk to enlighten the parent,

Orders, and

Pleading.

These writers say that most parents:

1. try to run their teenager's life;
2. fail to make their own lives happy.

They comment that parents impair their own happiness by assuming that they are entirely in charge of the child's actions and viewing the teen as incapable and irresponsible. That causes parents to lay aside their own needs and sacrifice their own happiness to be available to meet the teen's needs.

Use Direct Statements

Weinhaus and Friedman suggest that the parent start replacing questions with direct statements. For example, Mother agreed to do her son's laundry, but he sometimes rushed in at the last minute, thrust a load into her hands, and got angry with her when it wasn't ready on time. She asks: "Why don't you bring your laundry in earlier?"

A statement would be better: "I will do any laundry that you bring me by 9:30 at night. Otherwise you must do it." (And stick to it!)

Loosen Control

Change your focus.

Old focus: What the teen did. What can I do?

New focus: What I can do. What should my teen do?

If a parent takes responsibility for the teen's tasks, the teen, rather than feeling grateful, may become more demanding; the parent winds up feeling resentful and angry. The two get locked into a battle of wills.

The teen needs to take charge of his own tasks so he can develop skills and feel proud when he completes those tasks. One way to show love is to have faith enough to turn loose.

One father said to his sixteen-year-old son, "I've done everything

I know to make you clean up your room, and nothing has worked. I give up." The son cleaned his room.

A father took control of his daughter's homework: set up study hours, restricted her TV watching, and telephone time. She thwarted him by failing to turn in the work and "forgetting" to bring home assignments. He finally said, "I want you to do well in school, but I cannot force you to. I know you are intelligent and can do the work and I trust you to take charge."

When the parent backs away from controlling, the teen may try to bait the parent to get her back into "harness." The parent needs to know that this is normal and she needs to stay firm. When my middle daughter was thirteen, we moved and she entered a new junior high school. She had difficulty completing her homework so I took charge, supervising her the entire evening. After a couple of months, I sat down and said directly, "Both of us are unhappy with my involvement in your homework, so I'm going to turn it over to you."

A week later she came to me and asked me if I would take up the reins again. I refused but reentered the picture later when she did not turn in a large poster that she had worked hard on. "You said you would stay out," she reminded me and did not turn in the poster. As I recall, I "waffled" during her remaining high school years.

When she came home for the summer at the close of her freshman year in college, her grades showed a failure in religion. She had a block against doing term papers, and the lack of that paper gave her a failing grade. "I want to go to a local college this fall so you can take charge of my studies. If I'm going out to a party, you could say, 'Why are you going out when you have a test tomorrow?' " That time, I remained firm and told her that we were not going to go backward, that her college work was up to her.

When the parent stops askings questions, especially the accusing type, the teen usually starts asking them. This is how this developed with one mother and her son. The boy was not doing well in his schoolwork. Mother had asked the usual questions: Why aren't you doing your work? Don't you want to get a good job when you get older? and so on. She visited his teachers and got their agreement that she would stop any home supervision.

Jack came in one afternoon asking if he had any mail. Mother gave him a unopened letter. It contained a notice from school. She told Jack that a teacher called to report that he had failed to turn in three assignments that week. Jack gave a typical excuse, that he meant to do them and didn't have time.

Mother responded by saying she had felt upset at first because it looked as if he would have to go to summer school. Jack asked what she was going to do about it.

"I don't know," she said. "I understand that you feel pressured. I want you to do well in school, but you are the only one who can do the work. I will help you in any reasonable way but I will no longer supervise your homework. I know you will do what's good for you."

Let us review what Mother did.

She *described* without emotion—the letter came and the teacher called.

She *stated her feelings and thoughts.*

She *gave information about possible consequences.*

She *acknowledged his feelings.*

She *offered help.*

She *turned over the responsibility.*

She *expressed trust.*

She *set her own limits.*

How can a parent follow the above guidelines when the teen gets involved in serious matters, such as sex and drugs?

Ultimately, a parent cannot control a teen's behavior in those two areas. The teen is gone from home too many hours in a day for the parent to personally prevent those things from happening. And, if the teen wants to use either as a weapon against the parent, the more the parent tries to control, the more the teen will move toward that activity.

If the teen gets involved in either of those, the parent can allow him to reap the consequences of his activity. If he gets arrested for drunk driving, let the legal process play itself out and do not bail him out. Police arrested a minister's daughter for drunk driving and phoned her home. Both parents went into the police station at 4:00 a.m.

"Reverend, we know both of you, so we're going to let you take your daughter on home and we won't book her."

"No," the minister said. "You treat her the way you would any other offender." He and his wife assured the daughter of their support and made no judgmental statements to her, but they did not use their influence to spare her.

If parents learn a daughter is having sex with a boyfriend, family counseling is desirable. In that setting, each side can express feelings of hurt, disappointment, and anger. The daughter may choose to stop using sex as a weapon to hurt her parents. They can set their limits: She must not have sex in their home, and if she becomes pregnant they will not put their lives on hold to raise the child.

A couple, Mickey and Janet, discussed that the fact that their seventeen-year-old daughter, Stephanie, was having sex with her boyfriend. They tightened their control, made threats, delivered ultimatums, and talked against the boy. The family then went into counseling. In that setting the parents, both ACAs, spoke of their hurt, fears, and values in a person-to-person style with their daughter, and turned loose their child. Within a short time, the daughter started to see flaws in the boy and broke up with him.

Set Up New Behaviors

Weinhaus and Friedman say, "Be patient with yourself when you start changing the way you relate to your teen. Remember that it took your child many years of practice to become such an expert at giving excuses when you ask him to do something."

They give an outline for setting up new behaviors for your teen:

1. Tell what you want and state your willingness to negotiate. For example: "I want a different plan for you to eat dinner. Now, you come in when you want to and I leave dinner out and I feel annoyed. I want us to work out a new arrangement together."

2. Outline what you think would be a fair arrangement. For example: "I think it would be fair if I hold dinner thirty minutes and then I will put it away."

3. Negotiate and agree, using input from both of you. For example:

"If you come in later, you will get out your own food and clean up your dishes."

The important thing will be for the parent to stick to her side of the bargain. Her son may come in looking tired or down, and she might feel sorry for him and say to herself, "Well, just this once." If he complains about the lack of supper, she can remind him of their agreement.

What happens if the teen does not keep a contract that calls for him to do a specific task that affects the parent's life, such as not putting away groceries and food spoils? The parent can cut back on the services he provides the teen, such as doing his laundry, cooking his meals, taking him places. Inform the teen of your plan in direct statements: "I'm annoyed that you are not putting away the groceries as agreed, so I will not cook dinner for you for one week."

Humor works well with all ages but especially with teens. When he delays putting away his socks, threaten to hang them on the chandelier.

When a conflict gets underway between parent and teen, the parent can say: "Let's erase that and start over," using a sweeping motion. The parent can even go out of the room, reenter and take time to make an opening statement that will communicate more effectively.

Helping a Teenager Achieve Maturity

One father devised a plan to help his teenagers become independent at eighteen. J. D. Sanderson says that parents in middle-class American households coddle their children from birth onward and that if a child will be able to survive and prosper outside the family cocoon, "by age 13 a blast of cold air should be let in. The child must begin to see that not all of his needs are going to be tended automatically."

Sanderson advises instituting a realistic, four-to-five year plan for the child's final development into adulthood at eighteen or graduation from high school. Parents choose to turn responsibility over to the child and call on the child to take up the slack.

Sanderson and his wife introduced the concept of "Adult at Eighteen" to each of their children, Lisa, Eric, and Eve, on her or his thirteenth birthday.

"Five years from now," the parents said to the child, "you are going to be completely in charge of yourself. When you graduate from high school, it will be up to you to earn your own living. We will no longer support you." They made the following agreements with the child:

1. We're going to stop bugging you about your room.

2. We're going to stop worrying about your personal grooming. (This included giving advice about what to wear).

3. We are no longer going to tell you what time to go to bed. If you oversleep, we won't drive you to school.

4. We are not going to worry about what you eat.

Lisa, the first child, felt flattered and pleased with the new freedom, but also felt a bit anxious.

After six months, the parents called a second family conference. They praised Lisa's progress, then outlined three remaining areas in which changes would take place:

1. We expect Lisa to assume certain specific household responsibilities.

2. Whenever possible, Lisa will get where she needs to go on her own. We will no longer be instant chauffeurs.

3. When Lisa wants something, she will have to earn it.

Parents tend to get hung up on the question of providing their children a college education, Sanderson observes. "The most generous gift we can give high-school graduates is not a college education. It is the feeling that they have power and control over their lives," he says.

He gives these tips on how a young person can finance his own college education: teen savings; grants, scholarships, and/or loans; work for a year; work-study colleges; or college employment; parents' loans.

This plan, says Sanderson, states that parents seriously believe in their children's capacity to grow up and take care of their own needs. "All kids want to grow up and get control over their lives," Lisa affirms, "but nobody ever tells them how, or when."

While Sanderson's plan may not be right for all families, it does suggest options parents may want to consider in helping their teenagers make a successful transition to adult life.

Conclusion

Whatever the age of your children, your love for them expresses itself in your seeking help to enhance your effectiveness as a parent. An effective parent chooses appropriate parenting styles, maintains objectivity, communicates expectations clearly, and makes "I" statements. He or she allows children to participant in problem-solving, focuses on tasks and new behaviors. One of the most important things a parent can do is listen to his or her children.

Activities

Write in this book or use a separate notebook.

Building Self-Reliance in Children

Make a list of everything you do for your child(ren) during the day. Decide which ones must be done by an adult. Give to the child(ren) all that need not be done by an adult.

Adult required	Can be done by child(ren) Non-Life-Threatening Activities
_____	_____
_____	_____
_____	_____
_____	_____

Make a written contract with a child regarding some desired behavior. Describe the behavior in as specific terms as possible. For example, rather than say, "Be polite," define the activity you want. Build in consequences. Keep hands off when you observe the child either actively going off course or passively not staying on course. Apply the consequence at the end of the sequences rather than intervene and abort the process.

Desired behavior: _____

_____

Consequence: _____

_____

_____

Start Family Conferences

A teenage brother and sister got into a quarrel, and the brother pushed the sister against a door. The father "tackled" his son to bring an end to the conflict. The mother said: "We have to talk about this. In my alcoholic family, violence took place and nobody ever talked about their feelings."

The family—including the three teenagers—set up guidelines for a weekly family meeting.

1. They would meet each Sunday afternoon.

2. Every family member would be expected to attend and to stay for the entire meeting.

3. Members would be free to express any feelings, but they must observe guidelines for speaking: They must say, "I feel . . . ." rather than attack another with "You are . . . ."

This family reported remarkable improvement in family relations after following this custom for several months.

Change Your Behavior and Attitude

Write a self-contract outlining how you will change your behavior toward a child about whom you have a negative attitude. State it in positive, action terms. Read it once a day to yourself for twenty-one days. Visualize the child in an empty chair and read what you have written out loud to your "child." Notice his/her reaction in your imagination.

Child's Name: _____

My desired behavior change: _____

_____

Praise Diary

Keep a praise diary for one week, noting how many times you compliment, encourage, give positive strokes to your family members.

_____

_____

_____

_____

_____

_____

Evaluate Dinner Conversations

Tape two or three dinner conversations. Evaluate them according to the following questions.

1. Who talked the most? _____ .
   The least? _____ .
2. Who talked to whom? _____ .
   Did anyone avoid anyone? _____ .
3. Did family members make eye contact as they talked?   .
4. How much did members talk *at* each other (make speeches at, give advice, scold, etc.) rather than talk *to* (Use "I" statements and share feelings.) _____ .
5. How many SHOULD messages were given? (You shouldn't feel that way, You ought not to let that bother you, etc.)   .
6. How many *understanding* responses were given? (I understand how you feel, That must have been difficult for you, Tell me about it, etc.) _____ .
7. What roles were being acted out? _____ .
   Hero—taking care of others? _____ .
   Scapegoat—being the troublemaker _____ .
   Lost child—withdrawn _____ .
   Mascot—clown _____ .
8. Did members realy listen to each other or was there talking into space? _____ .
9. Did anyone make a request of another? _____ .
   If so, how? (Demand, complaint, accusation, or direct request? _____ .
10. Did anyone ask for information? _____ .
    How was the request handled? _____ .
    Was adequate information given? _____ .
11. Did anyone share a feeling? _____ .
    How did others respond? _____ .
12. Did anyone give someone else a mixed message? (Example: "Do this but do that." Contradictory messages.) _____
    _____ .

13. To what extent was the communication person-to-person rather than top-down? _____ .

14. Did any members seem to feel the need to defend themselves against one other member or the whole family? __.

Write a brief evaluation of your family's style of communication. Are you pleased with the way each member feels free to express himself/herself? Are you pleased with the way each responds to others?

What action, if any, would you like to take to increase the effectiveness of your family's communication? (Each person feeling free to share feelings with others without fear of being judged or rejected.)

Would you like to start making more "I feel" statements rather than telling others how to feel and act? (This style of communication draws people closer.)

10
The Path to Recovery

We have established the fact that as Adult Children from any type of shame-bound home we are immature. In seminars people ask, "What are characteristics of immature people?"

I answer jokingly, "To find out what is immature, look at your spouse!" None of us ever wants to admit to our own warts.

Maturity Our Goal

We, like Dorothy and her friends in *The Wizard of Oz*, are headed on a road (yellow brick or otherwise) to achieve maturity. Here is a list of characteristics that describe both maturity and immaturity.

Mature Person
1. Behaves assertively
2. Acts with compassion
3. Feels comfortable in many situations without compromising his values
4. Is growing; is open to new ideas and experiences
5. Acts rather than only talking, dreaming
6. Is hopeful and trusting
7. Is able to live by faith (includes religious faith and faith in a broader sense of being able to live with doubt, uncertainty, the unknown)

Immature Person
Behaves aggressively and/or passive/aggressively
Acts in punitive manner
Panics when meeting a new experience, idea, etc.

Is stagnant in personal growth

Acts passively, indecisively, paralyzed by fear of failure
Acts out of cynical viewpoint
Needs to control people and circumstances, needs to know all the answers before taking action

8. Is flexible, open to change viewpoint	Behaves in a rigid, dogmatic manner; there's one answer and he's got it and you should hold the same viewpoint; unable to change viewpoint with new input
9. Has self-confidence	Has difficulty trusting; behaves suspiciously and defensively; expects to be taken advantage of
10. Is integrated, whole	Compartmentalizes; has extremes in personality and behavior; is unreliable, unstable
11. Extends self	Acts in self-centered manner
12. Takes long-range view; thinks ahead and considers consequences of behavior	Behaves impulsively; acts in the moment
13. Views self realistically	Deludes self; has a lot of denial
14. Has unifying philosophy of life	Has too many loyalties (can't focus; heads in different directions at once, wastes energies)
15. Has harmious relationships with self and others	Has constant conflict with self and others
16. Sees changing oneself as key to improvement; focuses on responsibility for self-behavior	Sees changing others as key to improvement; focuses on trying to force others to change
17. Behaves in accepting, tolerant manner	Behaves in a critical and judgmental manner
18. Respects boundaries of others	Does not respect boundaries of others
19. Can operate within limits	Cannot accept limits
20. Has realistic view of cause and effect	Takes things personally, for both credit and blame
21. Maintains firm yet flexible personal boundaries	Has rigid, enmeshed, or non-existent boundaries
22. Operates out of integrity and morality	Does not operate out of integrity and morality
23. Able to delay gratification	Demands instant gratification

24. Able to control oneself   Unable to control oneself
25. Can share people, resources,   Jealous and envious
    and experiences
26. Trusting   Cannot trust
27. Humble   Excessively proud

Hurdles On the Way to Recovery

On the way to recovery, we encounter major obstacles in the form of hard realities of different types.

Change takes time.

Change takes practice.

Change cannot be rushed.

Change happens more quickly with the support of others with a similar goal.

Change happens in a two-step forward, one-step backward fashion.

We encounter obstacles in the form of our own feelings. Here are examples of the struggles Adult Children may have.

Some people fail to work through their hate and bitterness toward a parent who caused them pain. Their feelings consume them. In this case a person could join an Al-Anon group and learn principles of detatchment. Anger limits a person in many areas of life. Only when a person has put aside anger can she begin to view the parent with understanding and compassion. At this point, forgiveness is possible.

Others work through hate and anger, but cannot forgive a parent who has hurt them deeply and has since passed away. Unable to forgive, they cannot find peace with themselves. These people face the challenge of making peace with someone no longer living. In this type of situation, emotional closure is necessary. A therapist might suggest writing a letter expressing all the person's feelings. That letter could perhaps be read at the parent's grave. *Death does not make achieving closure impossible.*

Stages of Forgiveness

Terry Kellogg outlines stages in the process of forgiveness. "It is a process, not an event," he reminds us.

Stage 1: People recognize the wrong things that were done to them.

Stage 2: People recognize that they have feelings about those wrongs.

Stage 3: People embrace the feelings they felt about the abuse. Denied feelings are a psychological, physical, and spiritual drain that bring tension and stress to the body. Releasing feelings gives energy to make progress in recovery.

Stage 4: People share their feelings with others—sometimes the wrongdoer. Sharing lessens the isolation and reduces the hold that the abuse and abuser has over the lives of the victims. "Sharing with family requires judicious evaluation," Kellogg says. "Sometimes it may help heal. Other times we may get abuse in return, or the family denial will again break our hold on reality. Some family members may be too fragile (but less often than many of us believe) or may be no longer available. The process doesn't require direct confrontation because our goal is not to change others—only ourselves."

Stage 5: People decide what to do with the relationship with the abuser. The recovering person usually needs detachment which may call for a period of separation. Family members may give a lot of resistance at this stage because the recovering person is changing how he deals with the family. Kellogg says: "We often feel more guilty during this process, and it helps to remember that the guilt is a product of the family dysfunction. A healthy family encourages its members to do what makes them happiest."

When people have a better sense of themselves, they usually relate to their families on an improved level. Reconciliation is easier if the abuser has made positive changes.

Stage 6: People experience a feeling of serenity and acceptance about the wrong and the relationship with the offender. A person may still have feelings about the past, but those feelings no longer control him or force him into denial. A person may get started on recovery all over again when he becomes a parent or when he sees how he has hurt his children.

Kellogg concludes: "Recovery is a lifelong process of forgiving oneself and others."

Path to Recovery

We can do specific things to move us forward toward recovery:

1. Develop a spiritual program.
2. Get into therapy with:
   - a counselor who understands Adult Children issues,
   - a twelve-step program, or
   - both.
3. Get rid of all addictions to substances, including nicotine, caffeine, and food.
4. Develop a physical exercise program.
5. Develop healthy nutritional habits.
6. Develop a recreation program.

Develping a Positive Self-Image

You are the only self you've got. Someone said, "You could go back five thousand years and go forward five thousand and not find anyone just like you."

Jesus said that God knows the number of hairs on the head of each person, indicating our individual uniqueness. Fingerprints, voice patterns, and handwriting mark our individuality. With the self we respond to God. The more we discover our own uniqueness, the more we can respond to God in an authentic manner rather than copy another person's response.

Changing a Poor Self-Image

Many of us have a poor self-image. That is not God's desire. The Bible does not use the term *self-esteem*, but the value of the human being permeates the entire Scripture. The person who recognizes his true value is the one who can be truly humble. In *The Magic Power of Self-Image Pyschology*, Maxwell Maltz says:

> The greater the level of self-confidence a person has, the more he can practice humility. It is the person who has low Self-Esteem who puts on a false front of pretense and an air of pride. [The Bible calls putting on a false front *hypocrisy.*] There's only one corner of the universe you can be certain of improving, and that's your own self. Many of us give ourselves as much justice as would a lynch mob.

The aim is to find the best we have in us, realistically, and bring it out into the open. We do not attempt to create a fictitious self which is omnipotent or grandiose. Such an image is an untrue, inferior image.

According to Lee Milteer, a career development strategist:

> We have a mental image of who we are and what we are capable of. It can sabotage us or lead us to success.
>
> Too many people have the wrong message imprinted in the biocomputers that are their brains. We act out what we think of ourselves and we need to be aware that we often unconsciously carry negative opinions of ourselves and our capabilities that we have never questioned, never altered.

She says you can change your self-image for the better over a twenty-one-day period and "the results could turn your life around."

Use techniques of visualization and auto-suggestion to change your life.

> Choose one to three realistic, achievable priorities you want to work on. Every day for 21 days, right after you awake and right before you go to sleep, spend two to five minutes visualizing yourself achieving each priority. Be as vivid as you can—use emotion and your senses so that your subconscious will believe you. Also write out your priorities 21 times a day to fix your attention on them.

Autosuggestion comes next: "Seven to 21 times during the day, you must make positive statements, specifically backing up your visualization. Look in the mirror in the morning and say, for example, 'I, _____ _____, can handle anything today. I have tremendous energy today. . . .' You may feel silly, but your subconscious is paying attention!"

Make a master list from which to work. List thirty to fifty things you want to improve and tape record your list. Play the tape twice a day. Your subconscious will "buy" your voice and absorb what the tape is telling it.

Change the tape every thirty to sixty days, adding new statements or reading them in a different order. It takes single-mindedness and time to change your self-image.

Milteer advocates other techniques:

Use the hours you spend in your car as "university time." Pick an area of your life that needs strengthening and play a cassette of a list that covers it. "The mind absorbs what it hears repeated eight to 16 times."

Associate with positive, successful people and be a positive mentor to people around you: "Negative people are energy vampires," she says.

Use your support system—family, friends, coworkers—to bolster your self-confidence.

Visualize yourself as a successful person who can say no and who can take risks.

Our self-image defines the limits of our endeavors, the areas in which we must operate. Our beliefs and mental pictures predetermine the final results.

The subconscious is an automatic machine which responds to what we feed it—failure or success.

Maltz says:

> Your Self-Image will be strong only when you unlock the door to your human feelings. They are not so dreadful that you need to inhibit them constantly. If you think they are, it is your thinking that needs revision, not your feelings.
>
> If you bury your feelings deep inside you, you cannot have an accurate Self-Image because you cannot possibly know what you're really like. *You can only know what you're pretending to be.*
>
> When we over-conform, it distorts our Self-Image. You no longer really know who you are because you are always trying to please others. Bowing and scraping to please others will twist out of shape the unique qualities that make you an individual.When we overconform, we are not living our own lives at all. We are living someone else's—thus we're only partly ourselves.

Using Positive Self-Talk in Recovery

A recent newspaper article stated what I've been practicing for years: "It's healthy to talk to yourself!" What you say to yourself is extremely important. One person could feed negative thoughts and attitudes into his mind all day while another could do the opposite.

What do you say when you talk to yourself?

What is your style of self-talk? Failure?

"You can't ever do anything right. There you go again. You always mess up."

Or success?

"Yes, I've made some poor choices in the past, but I act more thoughtfully now, and I'm going to make it. I deserve good things in my life."

In the tape series, "The Inner Winner," Denis E. Waitley says, "Winning becomes a mental habit. Practice on the job. Act like a success outside the job. Imagine with words, roles, goals, and feelings what you want to achieve."

Waitley outlines steps to develop a success habit:

> Acquire knowledge
>
> Learn skills
>
> Internalize application of skills.

"When the mind talks, the body listens," he says. The body acts out what the mind thinks about. "We talk ourselves into and out of every defeat and victory of life," Waitley teaches.

The power of suggestion carries great power. When a person imagines an event, it compares to doing the actual thing. When a person who imagines running, for example, tiny contractions take place in the muscles that can actually be measured. The same process happens in every other area.

Waitley says:

> Each of us carries within us an "Inner Loser" or "Inner Winner" tape that is continuous loop, expandable, but nonerasable. By age 30 our tapes contain about three trillion messages about ourselves and our world. It records our self-talk minute by minute: several hundred words per minute with words, pictures and emotions. This becomes our Belief System."

Many of us write negative scripts for ourselves.

"I can't . . .

> do things well."
>
> do new things."

"Other people . . .

> don't like me."

don't like the way I look or act."

"Why try? It didn't work last time."

"Tapes in the minds of successful people say the following," according to Waitley:

"I like myself.

"I can try new challenges and be successful.

"If things don't go right the first time, I can try again or get new information to do it a different way."

Tap into the dialogues you have with yourself. We talk harshly to ourselves, condemning nearly every act. Self-talk creates self-image, and self-image governs and determines performance in every area of life, Waitley points out.

Everyone talks to himself automatically. We make most of our decisions based upon our real or imaginary experiences, fears, or desires based in our subconscious. We choose what we feed into our subconscious. We are constantly adjusting our self-image upward or downward. The self-image acts like a computer reading a disk and carrying out commands. We put the commands into that computer. We can put positive ones as well as negative ones.

Waitley says, "We usually become as successful as we plan to be." Our self-image expands and matures when we give positive, encouraging, and nurturing self-talk to ourselves.

We can use constructive forecasting in our self-talk each day. We can listen to inspirational tapes when we travel, bathe, and walk. We can read about people we admire who can show us the path to success.

Waitley warns that if we don't give ourselves affirmative directions, our minds and bodies will continue to take directions from anywhere or everywhere: fair-weather friends, envious peers, our own fears and doubts, bad TV news, print headlines.

Waitley gives these self-talk tips:

1. Listen to what you're saying to yourself. Construct affirmative self-talk statements.

2. Use present tense as if you've already achieved.

3. Always use personal pronouns and action modifiers: I, me, my.

4. Concentrate on incremental changes. Don't strive for perfection, just improvement.

5. Self-talk should focus on the habit you want, not the habit you want to break.

6. Combine general with specific self-talk. For example: All is well with me now. I save 10 percent of my pay check each month.

7. Each statement should be six to ten words in length, about four seconds.

8. Make a tape of your statements. Play soft, slow music in the background, repeating each statement three times.

9. Pick a time and place with privacy—just before sleep, early morning, or early evening.

10. Relax and breathe deeply as you listen to the tape. Visualize yourself with the goal already achieved.

Norman Vincent Peale says:

> Imaging consists of vividly picturing, in your conscious mind, a desired goal or objective, and holding that image until it sinks into your unconscious mind, where it releases great, untapped energies. It works best when it is combined with a strong religious faith, backed by prayer and the seemingly illogical technique of giving thanks for benefits before they are received. When the imaging concept is applied steadily and systematically, it solves problems, strengthens personalities, improves health, and greatly enhances the chances for success in any kind of endeavor.

In the activities section at the end of this chapter, you will find samples of self-talk to use as a guide to construct your own.

Realities About Recovery

Sharon Wegscheider says: "Surround yourself with people who will support your journey.

"Before we can move into any high self-worth place, it is important for us to ensure our daily living and safety needs. We need to be safe and comfortable: physically and financially."

One woman said that she takes inventory in what she calls the "five intimacies" of her life:

spiritual—meetings, meditation, fellowship;

emotional—exchanges daily love letters with her spouse;

intellectual—tries to keep up with current events;

financial—has a yearly budget, watches credit usage; and physical—diet, exercise, a yearly vacation.

Robert Subby says, "By recovering you innately become a therapist to the world. You reflect a new way of life and the courage to attempt it. Others who are hungry for that see it as a beacon of light, something to hang onto."

Philip Oliver-Diaz and Patricia O'Gorman write:

> We are all holding on for dear life to what we feel safe with, asking for help but unwilling to let go and let God. Even though our self-will often gets us in trouble, letting go is one of the hardest things for us to do. It goes against everything that we have learned as children.
>
> For adult children of traumatic families, reaching out to God and letting go feels like falling into an abyss. For many of us it feels like we are going to die. We have been taught to be self-sufficient *at all costs* and to trust only in our will to make things happen. Our trust in our will and the belief that we are alone in the world leaves us secretly bitter and hopeless, though the world rarely sees that face.
>
> We are taught to keep secrets, even from God. We are taught that sharing ourselves and our personal lives with others is bad and dangerous.
>
> *The reality is we cannot live without help.* Our unwillingness to lean on God and others for help has left us hopeless and exhausted, and sometimes physically ill. Our inability to reach out and become vulnerable has made it impossible for us to find fulfillment emotionally or sexually. And finally our anger at God has left us floundering in despair for meaning in our lives beyond sheer survival.
>
> The first step to entering the world is to reach out to God. Once we let God in, we become willing to let *people* come closer as well. Letting go of our hate and resentment and the hard pain that comes with those feelings; and allowing the soft pain of our mourning to wash over us is part of how we can love our inner child, and help her heal. Going in the direction of God's will, will create bridges for us to cross over of love, fellowship and forgiveness.
>
> By learning to trust, reach out and ask for help can we begin to turn the valve of living back on.

A thirty-year-old man stood by his mother's grave, holding a note neatly tucked into a plastic bag. Had Mother really died of cancer as the doctor had claimed or from her alcoholism? He remembered the sexual harassment he had suffered as a child. She did not remember the incidents, and the family members denied that it had happened.

As a child, he had learned to stuff his feelings, controlling them at all costs. Breaking out of this survival behavior from the home had been the most painful aspect of his own process of recovery.

He took the small plastic bag containing the note with his final words of forgiveness and good-bye, and with a small shovel he dug a hole deep into the dark earth by her grave marker. As he placed the note into the earth and buried it, a deep feeling of peace and serenity swept over him. He felt a great weight lift off his shoulders. He was free at last!

Activities

In a separate notebook or in the space provided, complete these activities.

1. Describe your reactions to your own first name.

For example: pride, delight, contentment, shame, embarrassment, hatred, resentment, anger, confusion, dislike, jealousy.

_____

_____ .

2. Name three animals you would like to be and three characteristics of each that you admire.

_____

_____

_____ .

What does that tell about you?

_____

_____

_____ .

3. List the names of three people you admire and three qualities of each.

_____

_____

_____ .

What does that tell about you?

_____

_____

_____ .

4. Write three wishes.

_____

_____

_____ .

What do these wishes tell about you?

_____

_____

_____ .

5. Write your five most important values.

_____

_____

_____ .

_____

_____ .

6. Take a look at your "I deserves. . . ."
   Start writing "I deserve . . ." and see how long a list you compile.

_____

_____ .

7. Picture an event that went badly.
   Re-create it, handling it successfully.
      Evaluate: Was it easy or hard? What roadblocks did you experience?

_____

_____ .

8. Recall the happiest experiences in your life. Evaluate. What elements were present?

_____

_____ .

Complete the following statements:
   1. Life is _____
   2. Others are _____
   3. I am _____
   Evaluate the responses. What patterns appear? What expectations have you set up?

_____ .

   By age seven, the Child creates a life plan, a belief system. We carry this self-image throughout life even though reality changes.
Write: At about age seven, I felt this way about:
   Myself:

_____
_____
_____ .

Others:

_____
_____
_____ .

The world:

_____
_____
_____ .

Life:

_____
_____ .

We view ourselves, others, and experiences based primarily on the viewpoint we had as a child and reject information that does not fit with that viewpoint. To what extent have your views changed since you were a child?

_____
_____
_____ .

In the following areas:
1. Are you OK or not?
2. If not OK, why?
3. What can you do to be OK?
   Social _____

_____
_____
_____ .

Emotional _____

_____
_____
_____ .

Physical _____

_____

_____

_____ .

    Intellectual _____

_____

_____

_____ .

    Spiritual _____

_____

_____

_____ .

    Recreational _____

_____

_____

_____ .

Write one flaw on paper.

    Burn the piece of paper and picture that flaw disappearing.

  9. Construct positive self-talk statements in all of the significant areas of your life:

    a. Relationship to self:

      Examples: I am a worthwhile human being.

               I enjoy myself.

               I am worth other people knowing.

    b. Relationship to spouse or intimate partner:

      Examples: I treat him/her with consideration.

               I listen attentively to him/her.

               I release him/her to have a separate identity.

    c. Relationship to a child:

      Examples: I deal effectively with my child.

               I think before I speak to my child.

               I take time each day to enjoy my child.

    d. Work:

      Examples: I am a valuable worker.

               I do my work with integrity.

               I respect boundaries at work.

    e. Recreation:

Examples: I value recreation in my life.
I give time and money to recreation.
I enjoy being good to myself.

f. Spiritual:
Examples: I value my relationship with God.
I take time for spiritual nurture.
God is my partner in all I do.

g. Financial:
Examples: I handle money wisely.
My spending habits are balanced.
I invest money for my future every month.

h. Personal Growth:
Examples: I am growing every day of my life.
I give time and money to personal development.
There are no limits to my growth.

i. Other

10. Use the recovery chart on the next page as a daily checklist:

STAMAS RECOVERY CHART

OLD SELF	NEW SELF
Feeling bad about self	Look at positive self. Accept compliments.
Mind-reading	Checking things out.
Overreacting	Understanding behavior. Looking at alternative behavior.
Looking at relaxation time and free time as boring, do-nothing or depressed time	Time for self Energy building time.
Just talking about problems over and over (no resolution)	Look at new behavior. Look at choices. Don't think about it – do it.
Over-controlling	Allow self to be taken care of. Express hurt instead of anger.
Over-committing	Saying No. Setting limits.
Giving and not receiving for self	Ask for nurturing. Give to self. Balance 50% giving and 50% receiving.
Hold resentments (marries you emotionally to that person)	Express anger effectively. Forgive person. Let go.
Guilt (self punishment) Not doing what you want to do	Forgive self. Do things that you want to do.
Fantasizing what you want to do	Do it.
Angry at loss of dream	Talk about loss. Grieving is letting go of dream.
Use illness to slow down	Make time to slow down. Provide fun time.
Exhausted feeling	Avoid over-committing. Recharge batteries.
Right/wrong – good/bad attitude	Develop comfortable/ uncomfortable attitude.
Sarcastic behavior	Talk about the hurt and fear.
Depression	Express anger. Don't internalize. Reach out and help.
Looking at others to determine how one feels	Be own thermometer.

Epilogue:
Co-Dependency and
Christian Living

On the surface, co-dependency messages sound like Christian teachings.

"Co-Dependents always put others first before taking care of themselves." (Aren't Christians to put others first?)

"Co-Dependents give themselves away." (Shouldn't Christians do the same?)

"Co-Dependents martyr themselves." (Christianity honors its martyrs.)

Those statements have a familiar ring, don't they? Then how can we distinguish between Co-Dependency, which is unhealthy to Co-Dependents and their dependents, and mature faith, which is healthy?

Co-Dependency says:

I have little or no value.

Other persons and situations have all the value.

I must please other people regardless of the cost to my person or my values.

I am to place myself to be used by others without protest.

I must give myself away.

If I claim any rights for myself, I am selfish.

I must repress all feelings.

Jesus taught the value of the individual. He said we are to love others *equal* to ourselves, not more than. A love of self forms the basis for loving others. The differences between a life of service and Co-Dependency take several forms.

- Motivation differs. Does the individual give his service and himself out of *free choice* or because he considers himself of no value? Does he seek to "please people"? Does he act out of guilt and fear? Does he act out of a need to be needed (which means he actually uses the other person to meet his own needs; the helpee becomes an object to help the helper achieve his own goals).

• Service is to be an active *choice.* The person *acts;* Co-Dependents react.

• Co-Dependents' behavior is addictive rather than balanced. Addictions control the person instead of the person being in charge of her own life.

• Co-Dependents have a poor sense of boundaries; they help others inappropriately (when it creates dependency on the part of the other person rather than moving that person toward independence.) They have trouble setting limits for themselves and allow others to invade their boundaries.

• A Co-Dependent's sense of self-worth is tied up in helping others; Christianity says that a person has worth simply because he is a human being God created. One's self-worth is separate from the work one does or the service one renders.

• Co-Dependents have difficulty living balanced lives; they do for others at the neglect of their own well-being and health; Christian faith calls for balanced living and taking care of oneself.

• Co-Dependent helping is joyless; Christian service brings joy.

• Co-Dependents are driven by their inner compulsions; Christians are God-directed and can be free from compulsiveness, knowing that God brings the ultimate results. Co-Dependents take full responsibility for the outcome of events; Christians do their work and recognize that results come from God.

• Co-Dependency is perfectionistic and merciless; God is merciful.

• Co-Dependency creates a religion of works; Christianity is a religion of grace.

• Co-Dependents feel filled with guilt and shame; Christianity says that God has removed our guilt.

• Co-Dependents do not have much actual faith in God; they have a pseudo-faith (genuinely consider themselves to have faith), yet have low trust in God; on a deep level, they view God as hostile and uncaring and model this type of God before others; the heart of Christian faith is trust in God.

• Co-Dependency is judgmental and gives conditional love; Christianity teaches that God gives us unconditional love.

• Co-Dependency causes people to allow others to treat them insultingly; Christianity teaches the dignity of every human being.

• Co-Dependency says we exist only and totally to serve others; Christianity teaches that we have value within ourselves and that it is not only *OK* to do things for ourselves, we *must* do that if we develop as mature spiritual beings.

• Co-Dependency rejects, and Co-Dependents are closed; Christianity accepts and leads people to be open.

• Co-Dependency causes people to try to control others and to try to force people to "do right"; Christianity teaches that we respect others' rights to be self-directing.

• Co-Dependency is black-and-white; Christianity stresses acceptance and respects differences.

• Co-Dependency is manipulative—service is rendered with some thought of gain (even if it is to make the servant feel good); Christian service is given without thought of gain.

• Co-Dependency leads to repression of feelings; the Bible teaches that God created us as beings who have feelings.

• Co-Dependency sacrifices individuals for the sake of the system; Christianity values the individual.

• Co-Dependency is hostile; Christianity is loving.

Activities

Make a list of the co-dependency styles of behavior, attitude, or feeling described in this chapter that you believe apply to you. Ask God to heal you and help your service to be Christian in spirit and in deed.

Bibliography

BOOKS AND ARTICLES

Beattie, Melody. *Codependent No More.* New York: Harper & Row, 1987.

Bradshaw, John. *Bradshaw On: The Family.* Deerfield Beach, Fla.: Health Communications, Inc., 1988.

_____. *Healing the Shame that Binds You.* Deerfield Beach, Fla.: Health Communications, Inc., 1988.

_____. "Our Journey Toward Wholeness," *Focus on Chemically Dependent Families,* April-May 1988.

Bresnahan, Maureen T. and Jeremiah B. "Family Boundary Systems," *Focus on Chemically Dependent Families,* Jan-Feb. 1985.

Burnside, Claire. "What Do We Mean by Abuse?" *Changes,* Sept.-Oct. 1987

Dunn, Jerry G. *God Is for the Alcoholic.* Chicago: Moody Press, 1965.

Dwinnell, Lorie. "Working Through Grief," *Focus on Family and Chemical Dependency,* May-June 1985.

Ellis, Albert. *Anger: How to Live With and Without It.* Secaucus, N. J.: Citadel Press, 1977.

Friel, John C. "Friel Co-Dependency Assessment Inventory," *Changes,* May-June 1985.

Friel, John C. and Linda D. Friel. "Family Stress and Recovery," *Focus on Family and Chemical Dependency,* Sept.-Oct. 1986.

Fossum, Merle A. and Marilyn J. Mason. *Facing Shame: Families in Recovery.* New York: W. W. Norton & Co., 1986.

Glenn, H. Stephen and Jane Nelsen. *Raising Children for Sucess.* Fair Oaks, Calif.: Sunrise Press, 1987.

Goodwin, Ray. "Free at Last," *Changes,* May-June 1987.

James, John W. and Frank Cherry. *The Grief Recovery Handbook.* New York: Harper & Row, 1988.

Kellogg, Terry and Mic Hunter. "Seeking Balance and Healthy Moderation, " *Focus on Family and Chemical Dependency,* Sept.-Oct. 1986.

Kritsberg, Wayne. *The Adult Children of Alcoholics Syndrome: From Discovery to Recovery.* Deerfield Beach, Fla.: Health Communications, 1986.

LeBoutillier, Megan. *Little Miss Perfect.* Denver: MAC Publishing, 1987.

Leman, Kevin. *Making Children Mind Without Losing Yours.* New York: Dell Publishing, 1984.

Lerner, Harriet. *The Dance of Anger.* New York: Harper & Row, 1985.

Lerner, Rokelle. *Daily Affirmations for Adult Children of Alcoholics.* Pompano Beach, Fla.: Health Communications, Inc., 1985.

Littauer, Florence. *Lives on the Mend.* Waco, Tex.: Word Books, 1985.

McKenna, David. *The Psychology of Jesus.* Waco, Tex.: Word Books, 1977.

Malone, Thomas Patrick and Patrick Thomas Malone. *The Art of Intimacy.* New York: Prentice Hall Press, 1987.

Maltz, Maxwell. *The Magic Power of Self-Image Psychology.* New York: Pocket Books, by arrangement with Prentice-Hall, Inc., 1970.

Martin, Sara Hines. *Healing for Adult Children of Alcoholics.* Nashville: Broadman Press, 1988.

Mets, Wally. *Deep River.* Denver: Accent Books, 1978.

Middleton-Moz, Jane. "Discovering the Discarded Self," *Focus on Chemically Dependent Families,* April-May 1988.

Newkirk, John O. "Workaholism: The Pain Others Applaud," *Focus on Chemically Dependent Families,* Aug.-Sept. 1988.

Oliver-Diaz, Philip and Patricia O'Gorman. "Parenting for Recovery," *Changes* Jan.-Feb. 1987.

Peale, Norman Vincent. *Positive Imaging.* Old Tappan, N. J.: Fleming H. Revell Co., 1982.

Peck, M. Scott. *The Road Less Traveled.* New York: Simon and Schuster, 1978.

Polson, Beth and Miller Newton. *Not My Kid: A Parent's Guide to Kids and Drugs.* New York: Avon Books, 1984.

Rubin, Theodore. *The Angry Book.* New York: Collier Books, 1969.

Samalin, Nancy. *Loving Your Child Is Not Enough.* New York: Viking Press, 1987.

Sanderson, J. D. "Adult at Eighteen?" *Reader's Digest,* Mar. 1977.

Sandford, John and Paula Sandford. *Healing the Wounded Spirit.* South Plainfield, N. J.: Bridge Pub., Inc., 1985.

_____. *The Transformation of the Inner Man.* South Plainfield, N.J.: Bridge Pub., Inc., 1982.

Seamands, David. *Healing for Damaged Emotions.* Wheaton, Ill.: Victor Books, 1984.

Shipp, Thomas J. *Helping the Alcoholic and His Family.* Englewood Cliffs, N. J.: Prentice-Hall, Inc., 1963.

Smalley, Sondra and Eli Coleman. "Addiction & Addictive Relationships," *Focus on Family and Chemical Dependency,* Jan.-Feb. 1987.

Spickard, Anderson and Barbara R. Thompson. *Dying for a Drink.* Waco, Tex.: Word Books, 1985.

Somers, Suzanne. *Keeping Secrets.* New York: Warner Books, 1988.

The Twelve Steps for Christians. San Diego, Calif.: Recovery Publications, 1988.

Stamas, Dene. "Recovery Chart," *Changes,* Jan.-Feb. 1987.

Waanders, David D. "Ethical Reflections on the Differentiation of Self in Marriage," *The Journal of Pastoral Care,* June 1987.

Weinhaus, Evonne and Karen Friedman. *Stop Struggling with Your Teen.* St. Louis: J. B. Speck Press, 1984.

Whitfield, Charles L. *Healing the Child Within.* Deerfield Beach, Fla.: Health Communications, Inc., 1987.

Woititz, Janet Geringer. *"Ask Jan,"* *Changes,* July-Aug. 1987; Nov.-Dec. 1987.

_____. *Struggle for Intimacy.* Pompano Beach, Fla.: Health Communications, Inc., 1985.

TAPES

Sandford, John. "Bitter Root Judgment," "Inner Vows," "Cutting Free," "Restoring Basic Trust." P. O. Box 722, Coeur D'Alene, ID 83814.

Sledge, Timothy D. "Adult Children of Alcoholics," Encouraging Word.

Waitley, Denis E. "The Inner Winner." Nightingale-Conant Corp., 7300 N. Lehigh AV, Chicago, IL 60648, 1- 800-322-55552.

NEWSLETTER

Elijah House Newsletter *(free)* P. O. Box 722, Coeur D'Alene, ID 83814.

Where to Get More Help

The following sources can give information about how to start a twelve-step group with a Christian approach for anyone who is interested in starting a group in a church.

Counselor
First Baptist Church
Euless, TX

Bob Bartosch
17027 E. Jamison Dr.
Whittier, CA 90603

Pastor
Chapel Hill Harvester Church
4650 Flat Shoals Rd.
Decatur, GA 30034

Dr. Timothy Sledge
Kingsland Baptist Church
20555 Kingsland Blvd.
Katy, TX 77450

Adult Children of Alcoholics
2522 W. Sepulveda Blvd. St. 200
Torrance, CA 90505
(213) 534-1815
Monday-Thursday 1:00-6:00 p.m.

To start an Al-Anon Adult Children's group, contact your nearest Al-Anon headquarters.

Al-Anon/Alateen Family Group Headquarters, Inc.
Madison Square Station
New York, N.Y. 10010
(212) 683-1771

Alcoholics Anonymous World Services, Inc.
468 Park Avenue South
New York, N.Y. 10016
(212) 686-1100

Co-Dependents Anonymous
P.O. Box 33577
Phoenix, AZ 85067-3577

National Association for Children of Alcoholics
31706 Coast Highway, Suite 201
South Laguna, CA 92677
(714) 499-3889

National Council on Alcoholism
12 West 21st Street
New York, N.Y. 10010

National Clearinghouse for Alcohol Information
P. O. Box 1908
Rockville, MD 20850
(301) 468-2600

The following ministers and/or counselors practice Inner Healing. They can help you or help you locate names of persons in your area who are trained to do Inner Healing.

Rev. and Mrs. Dennis Bennett
The Christian Renewal Asso.
P.O. Box 576
Edmonds, WA 98020-0576

Dr. David Seamands
115 Fairway
Nicholsville, KY 40356
(606) 858-3581

Francis and Judith McNutt
Christian Healing Ministries, Inc.
438 W. 67th St.
Jacksonville, FL 32208
(904) 765-3322

William and Carolyn DeArtega
2957 Lexington Trace Dr.
Smyrna, GA 30082
(404) 426-5257

John and Paula Sandford
P.O. Box 722
Coeur D'Alene, ID 83814